prickly garden

Gardens are beautiful . . . and roses have thorns!

Terry Walton

I have long loved knowing the names of the shrubs and flowers and that I see on my morning walks. Bill Barash - horticulturist, photographer, and friend - knows the common and Latin names of everything I see and have yet to see. Cover, from top: Roses, Goldenrod and Aster, Kordesii Rose, Japanese anemones.

©Terry Walton 2023
ISBN number 978-0-9711869-5-8
Rosalie Ink Publications
Box 291, Cold Spring Harbor, NY 11724
Designed by Eric Neuner
Printed by Rosemont Inc., Deer Park, NY

COVER PHOTOGRAPHS
Courtesy Bill Barash, Oyster Bay, NY

ACKNOWLEDGEMENTS

Prickly Garden thanks are quiet ones. Mine is a minor work, so here is a soft tune of gratefulness for friends who joined in along the way. Three years ago, still pre-covid, my friend Lynn Tone noted that in the weekly writings we exchanged, I could do with a little more grit and fewer mere musings on happiness. Hence the title *Prickly Garden* – which does reflect life, doesn't it?

For early encouragement I thank my family trio of Jenifer, Robert, and Bob. Also, Kaitlyn Pawlukojc, and Jeanie Tengelsen.

For art and design I thank graphic artist Eric Neuner, whose joyous emails buoyed the days, as well as Bill Barash for plentiful art help, and Bessie Fuchs and Audrey Halpern for theirs.

For vignette review en route I thank Walter Kolos, Peter Sloggatt, Michael Fairchild, and Liz Powers. And, Robert Ferraro for insightful comment on the poems. RSW

To Bob, a former federal prosecutor and
my husband of fifty-seven years, who encouraged
each of my adventures – Stonehenge, Easter Island,
Pitcairn Island, Galapagos, Africa, Great Lakes Geology,
Coast Guard helicopter flights out to Ambrose Tower
for the day for a story, a lovely lengthy list.
Dad and Gpa are his other beloved names.
He is the Bob mentioned in my *Prickly Garden* adventures.

INTRODUCTION

A Quitclaim: *Prickly Garden's* vignettes and poems are gathered as
"imperfect unedited words" (the author is the editor . . .). They come
from ordinary days – a flat tire in a downpour far from home, a walk
around the block noticing weeds and perfect lawns, the shared and
agonizing fear for our Earth and our children and their children.
Also, unexpected delicious "coincidences" that take my breath away.
And, despairing moments when politicians place self over country,
or when babies and strangers suffer. In fact rage and sadness have
danced through my own eighty-two years of life, bringing their
wisdoms and ultimately, beyond measure, gratefulness and joy.
Blessings abound.

ERIC NEUNER

Quietness

*Oh there is solace in the same old thing. In the quiet of morning,
storms of rancor and illness rage outside my cocoon of ordinariness.
Small things yield comfort beyond their customary selves. ∗ I see our dog lift
her head skyward for my fingers caressing beneath her chin. Hunch her shoulders
forward for my nuzzle at the nape of her neck. When I speak her ears swivel back
slightly, toward the sound of my voice. ∗ I fold the week's laundry unhurriedly,
aware of soothing textures, of the luxury of clean and safe, remembering
how my mother taught me to fold the towels in lengthy thirds and then in a half
and half again, the better to sit in good order on their shelf. ∗ I water a valiant
old cyclamen, brazen pink blossoms reaching toward light, aligned and bold
like little soldiers doing their morning march. I tend the cyclamen's sisters,
saying I'm sorry I'm sorry for the neglect that has caused their leaves to droop.
I am heartened by their forgiveness as they strengthen upright again. ∗ I turn off
the last light at bedtime, as I always do. The day's work is done. Some of its kindly
moments resurface now, as they always do just now. My pillow is a welcome,
and words blur on the pages of my book. I will sleep into tomorrow and
wake to sunrise, as I always do. ∗ Each day, if I pause to notice, holds these amulets
of a calmer time. Blessed reminders of habits sustained, threading through the
dreads of yesterday and today. And promising, in their steadfastness,
to stay by me in the coming days.* RSW

CONTENTS | *Vignettes and Poems*

Vignettes

Lost Loon	15
Why Three?	19
My Honorary Hungarian Uncle Frank	27
UCV – What's That?	32
Some Things Matthew Doesn't Know	40
Sailing in Her Basket Boat	43
Betrayal Is a Big Word!	47
Summertime Visits in My Neighborhood	55
Twice Shy	58
As Old as December	61
Living With Richard and Emeline	65
Mr Robinson's Silver	69
Stranger Story Foolishness	76
Lovely Laundry	81
Esmeralda	88
The Girl in the Blue Dress, Dancing	95
Spathy & Philo	100
Whatever Happened to Alice and Fredrica?	109
Ali & George	113
Anchorages	117
Tell Me True, Damn It!	121
Trumpet Vine Time	124
Strawberries	128
Honor the Upstarts of the Season	134
Oh, the Irony of Vision – Eternal 2020	136
Oh, Little Did I Know – The Way Out 2021	138

CONTENTS | *Vignettes and Poems*

As Silvered Elder / What Should I Do Now? 141
Seven Self-Servings of the Good Stuff 148
Mr Forsyth's Forsythia 153
My Morning Walk 156
Goings and Comings 163
Stanley Smiled 168
The Lightening 171
They Taught Me How to Love 172

Poems

Church at Home 18
Comfort 18
Weeds 22
Hope 23
Despair 23
Skateboard Boy 24
October 25
Spring Rain Outside the City 26
Metaphors 30
Clover 31
Leaf Blowers 36
Sound 37
Grandmother 37
Noah and Andrew 38
Sand 39
Out East 42

CONTENTS | *Vignettes and Poems*

Bathing	46
Found in October	50
Chores	51
Winds and Silences	52
Lexicon	53
Maples in Autumn	54
Rest	60
Spirit	64
Tiny Girl	68
Common Cold	72
Love	73
St John's Church	73
No One	74
Vermeer	75
Beautiful Tree	75
Take Notice	80
One More Thing	84
Should	85
Fresh Grace	86
Why?	94
Muddled 2020	104
The Old Ways 2020	105
Corona Solo	106
2020 Mother	107
A Walk 2020	108
Ode to Coffee Grounds	112
My Bower	116
Aging in Place 2020	120

Toy Basket 2020   120

CONTENTS | *Vignettes and Poems*

Privilege   126
Low Morning 2020   127
How Is It . . .   132
Ladies of Leisure of Yore   133
Openness   140
Earth   144
Go-to-Hell Friday   145
Love II   146
Azaleas in November   147
Boy and Ducklings at St John's Pond   152
Out for a Walk Today   160
Dirt Resplendent   161
After a Time of Tears   162
Aging in Place II   166
Check the Trees for Squirrel Nests!   166
The Dancing Leaf   170

Lost Loon

Eudemonia disappeared one day and I survived! Never thought I could or would, but the years of "making peace with the what is" and noticing everyday miracles – in which she played a quiet starring role – kicked in. Eudemonia is a tiny wooden loon, carved with affection and painted with care. Each feather, each curve, is honored in delineation of quiet colors – greys, browns, blacks, touches of white. Her friends in the wild, size aside, would never know the difference. Her carver was a meticulous man; I met him once long ago.

To me she is an amulet, a friendly presence at morning coffee time, at ponder-things-and-plan-the-day time. She sits beside my favorite chair, beak a little broken and paint dimmed, or had done so for close to forty years. This time, however, grandchildren, those curious, admiring beings, must have changed her customary place and she was lost. Weeks went by, searches in and around, under and over, gone.

Why an amulet? Family illnesses year after year, fear for a child in crisis, cold anxiety for whither from here, the whole world in trouble – comfort and calm missing in this string of stresses, yet deeply needed. Eudemonia means "happiness in a rational life," I read somewhere. Euphoria over demons. Hence the name, the gift so needed in a string of scares.

One in the string began with panic attacks and ultimately a year of psychiatry and tranquilizers. A museum director had hazed me with anonymous little blue notes on my desk, then reassigning my projects to incompetent others, and giving me assignments and saying he had not. All spiced with dressing me down in all-staff meetings. He finally fired me "at will" with pleased evil in his eyes. Psychopath.

An ER doctor prescribed new medication. I took it. Gone was confidence, gone was joy. Not a shred of either. New to me was a bizarre fear of being alone, of venturing anywhere at all.

"Come to the Knicks game with us," said husband and son one day.

"I can't," I said.

"Call a friend to come over," they said.

"I can't."

Sobbing at the drop of a hat. I who have traveled solo far away many a time.

Time and modified medication fixed things. But after the siege my first trip outdoors alone was to a local wildlife festival, minutes away. The carver was there. I made it to festival and back – triumph. A small momentous thing.

Eudemonia has tiny penciled dates on her little body – 1992, the panic time. 2002, hope for the safety of a child. Next prayers (answered) for the first grandchild soon to come. Then six years ago emergency save-foot-leg-life surgeries for spouse. More things since as I neared age eighty.

Eudemonia had seen me through all. From her presence came my saving grace behavior: Get tidy. Write it all down if you have to. "The worst that can happen is this [dreaded outcome], in which case here's what I'll do [name a clear next step]." A survivable plan in place.

Joy figured with Eudemonia too. Seeing a maple leaf skip magically along beside me in light afternoon wind. A praying mantis hidden openly on the front yard rhododendron. Pink morning sky presaging a good day. Memory of little grandchild hands reaching out to me, and the wondrous "Gma!" sound. And more. Glory be.

Yet Eudemonia, witness to all these pendulum fears and elations, was gone. Search beneath papers casually tossed. Fingers finding empty dust under the old radiator. Move everything, search under and over a second time, last search again next day. She was well and truly gone. I made peace with even this, a betrayal of peace hard won.

Early mornings unaccompanied. Time to think about this. Eudemonia was not born my amulet, she became it. What else around the house might I learn to love this way? What's out there for me to come upon unhurriedly and recognize as Eudemonia's successor? Could I envision a mental trek with clearing light at the end of it?

Yes. Peace came back to me – in the teachings of time and my absent amulet. And so, weeks later and dusty from her time beneath the old radiator, did Eudemonia.❖

Church at Home

Sacred Sunday time
Time set aside for gratefulness
Wondering, pondering, quietness
For love letters, thirsty plants
For gathered intentions
For spirit-strength, ineffable.

Comfort

Oh, such comfort lies
In the familiarities of morning
Amidst the chaos of the world.
First coffee, sunrise, quietness,
Then walk along neighborhood streets,
Ponder life, notice all the shades
And stages of green – light, deep.
Then tend my own plants, and
Begin a new day of ordinary tasks.

Why Three?

An engaging semi-drunk Columbia University professor started the whole thing years ago – my enduring affection for the number 3. The Greeks, he told us, poured out their libations three times to find favor with the gods. Need rain? Tip the goblet three times. Succeed in war or politics? Tip three times more. The Greeks must have sown hope in this tried-and-true way of theirs, and their custom came to make sense to me, even give comfort at dire or hopeful times.

The professor taught Greek drama at Columbia at night. I subwayed up there after work that year, first interested in the Greeks for reasons unremembered sixty years later. I had blown away prestigious college in Massachusetts and now worked in the MacMillan Publishing steno pool by day for pittance. Then rushed uptown on the Lex for college credits at 5:30 pm - engergized by sugar packets stolen from the local McDonald's at lunch.

I forget his name, the professor, but I can still see him striding harassed and headlong into class. Sweat glistened his face as he made it to his desk. Alcoholic or not, this man did really light up my love for Greek plays. And thus, gift me some lasting understandings.

"Wisdom through suffering," for instance. The Greek dramas we read all seemed to end with enlightenment after turmoil. The Greek people went to see their plays over and over again, I gathered, finding solace in their own anguishes being mirrored and resolved every time. And when one day I did find myself at a Greek amphitheater in Athens, I climbed the steep steps all the way to the top, to sit alone on rock-hewn seats, envisioning taking comfort there as the Greeks once did. Envisioning taking comfort, and *actually* taking it. My life had some conundrums of its own.

The Greek libation tradition did sway some playful behaviors for me. My car license plate has long been Ter333, and my computer passwords all seem to stem from there. My first password had 33 in it – obediently changed up and up to ward off hackers, and always to my age so I wouldn't forget the password. The last time was 65. By rights it should be 80 today; I missed 75.

Today I add three smidgeons of brown sugar to my morning oatmeal – ceremony inviting a good day. A large hand-scrawled number 3 is taped to the French door near the chair in which I have morning coffee. It has been there for years, telling me to intend three kind things or count three blessings to start the day. It works oddly well. Counting blessings is always a good thing – especially, I have learned, when the sky is falling.

I tried engaging my dour retired-lawyer life-partner in this three-blessings thing, but without avail. Well, that's ok; it's my thing that I do. Many a morning begins in remedial philosophizing for me – some quiet ideas and plans yielding the way through.

Now and then I even discover earlier instances of three, as if predestining my evenings with the Greek drama professor: My brother's birthday was January 3. My father's January 23. My sister died on March 3. Our little family sailboat Windtoy growing up was #342. (From that I've even zagged sideways over to 342 and 242, my hospital room numbers as a new mother, or 12:42 birth time for our daughter, and 7:42 birth time for our son; but that's of course ridiculous. . . .)

More recently someone suggested, zow, that my "three" represented the holy trinity. Well, I sure never thought of that. But perhaps the Greeks and the Trinity are connected in this mystical way.

One really good thing about my "three" affection is that I've never felt OCD-compelled to pat the dogs three times for luck when I walk by, or knock wood precisely three times. Or do anything else at all – beyond pondering things over coffee, and enjoying the self-serving three smidgeons of sugar for my cereal.

It's just that where comfort suggests itself, I say – the comfort of ritual even as suggested by the Greeks forever ago – why not say thank you, yes, I need it, I'll take it. ❖

Weeds

In a walk after rain
I am dazzled
By the lushness of weeds
Richest spring green
Tall and proud as cornstalks.

Despair

How could I, of all people, feel despair?
I'm so sunny. I'm the soul of things, friends say.
So spirit-rich, so full of the cheering gift of friendship.
Well, I feel despair instead.
And I feel the fear of unknown things,
Way down deep and chest-ache strong, with it.

Hope

Leaves gone from trees in Fall?
A neighborhood tree
With rich complement
Of twigs and branchlets?
Why, it's perfect for squirrels' nests!
There's one –
There's another . . . and one more.
Good heavens:
Clever squirrels, blessed tree.

Skateboard Boy

Skateboard boy – happy shout, out of sight
Then I glimpse the pint-size blue-shirt person
Zooming down drive to street and back again
And again, executing artful turns.
I think of young neighbors, joy sounds, innocence,
Privilege not yet recognized. I think of the world
Around the skateboard boy, the world yet unbeknownst.
The world he will enter, join, help I hope.
The world of shootings, floods, fires, acts of God
And kindnesses, so many kindnesses.

October

Rain grey morning
Pleasing, cleansing hours of day
Glory sunset
Things turn out well.

Spring Rain Outside the City

Sometimes
When I am running through the sky
In Spring rain
(the sky is in the puddles)
I see earthworms – fleets of them –
Earnestly crossing, never looking.
It's hard on the ankles
To miss them
But I do!

My Honorary Hungarian Uncle Frank

Gruff voice, strong Hungarian accent, dear family friend – that's my forever recollection of Uncle Frank. I first knew him as a mysterious man who sailed all over the oceans and was "old like my parents." Which means he was likely about thirty-eight to my age seven. He sent me presents from everywhere it seemed.

One such present was an ebony letter opener – shapely blade, handsome African head the *objet* of the art. It lay safely in a drawer for sixty years. Then one day my customary letter opener vanished and Uncle Frank's ebony treasure emerged for its intended use.

The African man depicted is no ordinary man, he is Kingship. He is an honored noble of his continent with regal profile and hair carved in stately rows. The letter opener lives now beside my pens and pencils and scissors of everyday use, in a coffee cup that has lost its handle. I wish I could ask Uncle Frank where in Africa he found this gift, but after a long intercontinental seaman's life he has sailed into beyond.

Uncle Frank, I would learn as a child, was my honorary uncle. He met my father and actual uncle aboard the square-rigged ship *Tusitala*. He is the centerpiece of how my parents met each other and lasting friendships began – my mother Mariamne's brother Frederick, my father Henry, and Uncle Frank – sailors all. Frederick and Henry were "gentlemen sailors" aboard this near last remaining square-rigged ship. And Frank was hard young weathered crew who would one day captain Grace Line ships on all the world's oceans.

I kept in touch with Uncle Frank and his children for years, well into the time of my own marriage and children. He told me of leaving home at age fourteen to crew on a Baltic lumber schooner. Once he gave me his open oceans collection of negatives, large frame, because of my work as a maritime editor. In one of the prints Uncle Frank appears forever memorably for me – handsome and proud, shirtless, barefoot, pants legs rolled up, arms crossed and legs planted for balance. Towering rigging and shipmates in similar stances join him in the scene, which is likely an Equator crossing with the attendant foolishnesses. Clearly a different voyage from the gentlemen sailor sort.

Among Uncle Frank's photographs are some from the top of *Tusitala's* mast in a wild gale – waves crashing over the foredeck and roiling in the lee scuppers. They are remarkably sharp photographs for their day, and timewise they coincide with a ship's log in which her Captain Barker records the winds and daily routines of the vessel, crossing oceans with cargoes for hither and yon. *Tusitala* – whose name means teller of tales in Samoan – is an important ship in maritime lore for her own reasons, literary and obscure these days. But years ago I traveled West with noted maritime historian Norman Brouwer to interview Uncle Frank about his life and Captain Barker's log.

We learned, the historian and I, that Captain Barker had teased the hell out of my "gentleman sailor" Uncle Frederick for losing a leather bucket over the side. "The cost of the leather" Captain Barker began. "And the hours of labor to stitch it . . . and the braided handle . . . and the woven lanyard . . . the costs of replacement . . ." Uncle Frank smiled at the telling, and uproarious laughter overcame us at this memory. Imagine my horrified young Uncle Frederick (always stately and self-assured in my life) hearing how much he owed for this transgression. Captain Barker was known for his sharp tongue and appropriate name giving the ship's orders, so this tale of his playfulness

was especially fine. I still have the extraordinary negatives, and gifting them to a New York museum has escaped me for far too long. I have the taped interview too, and believe I know who still has the old ship's log.

Today I see Uncle Frank's noble-African letter opener and I think back to its era as a gift, when I was seven or so and he came to visit my parents. He sent me other gifts too – and likely some to my brother and sister as well, but I don't remember those. And everyone is up there somewhere sailing with Uncle Frank now, so I cannot ask them.

I think back to how handsome Uncle Frank was in those photographs. I think further back to our family rumor that he cared much for my mother Mariamne for all of his life with his own wife and children. And I see the tiny cerulean-blue tea cups with copper handles that he sent me – these from China – with a copper pitcher, part of a little girl's tea set. And I see the small Navajo rug that is long worn through, just fourteen inches wide or so and less than twice that in length. He lived in Montana, Uncle Frank did, and perhaps the tiny rug came from times there, home from the sea.

What I love to believe about all this, now that I am an elder older than my parents and Uncle Frank ever were, is that Uncle Frank, who never lost his rumbly Hungarian accent and his quiet smile, forever loved both my parents, perhaps my mother in particular in his way. And that perhaps the gifts to me and my brother and sister were part of that enduring affection for her. How lovely for my mother if so. ❖

Metaphors

I went for a walk of metaphors this morning
Merely for exercise, no metaphorical frame of mind.
Yet there they were all around –
Messages for the seekers of solace.
A new trellis at a lamppost, clematis just planted
Purple and eager to climb. Bright pink azalea
Trimmed tight to hedge shape, surely against its will.
Lush lilies of the valley, annual streetside swath
Of elegant white on green, shaded, luxuriant
Six or seven bells to the stem. And so forth.
Familiar nature, streetside and friendly.

Clover

Today I saw bravery at lawn's edge –
Miniature clover clusters defied a whirling whacker's
Stark task trimming inches of soil and sod.
The trimmer, one of those lethal slicers
Favored by perfect lawn-keepers,
Could not defeat the boldness I saw there.
I saw a whole fresh colony of clover, miniatures,
A baby-clover carpet thriving at street's edge,
Cascading four inches past the tidy lip of the lawn.
Go, clover!

UCV – What's That?

UCV? Google has solved one mystery and touched off another. My father Henry was a handsome man. A gentle man. A gentleman. Quiet voiced, raised a Quaker, thrown out of Princeton in '26, a cousin once told me, for prioritizing Newport house parties over academics. He was comfortable at City clubs and country clubs. Meanwhile my mother Mariamne was borrowing stockings from friends at Smith College, and left when her scholarship ran out; she was unsure if her parents had enough to eat. My parents had yet to meet.

Young Mariamne was beautiful, I see from sepia society-page rotogravure from her day. And young Henry looked innocently dashing in his black Coast Guard uniform of brass buttons and formal white-visored cap. They had both lost the luster of youth by the time I entered life, but I am told that their marriage was one of lasting love and I believe it. Theirs was not a marriage of visible hugs and embraces. Their ways were otherwise and their own. A smile, a touch on the shoulder, a fond tone in their conversations with each other. I never heard my father raise his voice.

Hovering widows and two stepmothers followed Mariamne's death (four years ill, death finally at fifty-one). My first stepmother died, another ineffable sadness for my father, and the second one was drunk at their wedding and most of the time thereafter; I choose to believe that they had some happy times together. Henry himself left this earth more than thirty years ago at the "venerable age" of seventy-eight. Too soon for anyone, now that I am well past there myself. Seventy-eight is not a venerable age. It is a vibrant age and his death was too soon. How I wish I could ask him a million things right now.

I received my father's effects – from Mariamne's side or Henry's side I have not yet discovered – letters from the 1800s, the family wedding veil presumed lost after my own wedding a lifetime ago, some sailing logs (Henry sailed transatlantic and did the Bermuda Race with friends), and other unexplored treasure still in a large flat cardboard box. And also, an odd-shaped brass medal dangling from a hook marked Souvenir. I remembered it merely as "UCV" and just let it be for a time, beneath some notes on a table beside my go-to chair.

The day came when I held the medal to the light and had a lingering look. Its tiny words are arranged around a square in orderly incised block letters, top and bottom, left and right, as if at noon, three, six, and nine on a clock: REUNION at the top, then JUNE and 1-2-3 reading up vertically at left and right, and the date 1915 down at six o'clock. Inside, in a neat block-letter circle reading clockwise around an inner enameled red and blue square, are the words UNITED CONFEDERATE VETERANS RICHMOND, VA. The medal is more than a century old – meticulously designed and only slightly shimmery, a squared shape with deep square-ended notches in its corners. Thanks to magnification and splendid light, I deciphered "Schwaab S&S Co. Milwaukee" stamped in miniscule letters on the back. Schwaab Stamp and Seal Company, per the Numismatic Bibliomania Society website, "made a type of badge different from all others that collectors call a 'stamp and stencil medal.' It is uniface, struck on sheet brass, often of an unusual shape and without any patina." The medal became for me a small mysterious treasure.

I looked it all up online and there it was: yes, United Confederate Veterans, the explanation for my forgotten acronym UCV. The red and blue enamel is a showing of the Confederate flag, and the singular shape the

South's version of a Maltese cross, known as the Southern Cross. Lettering confirms the June 1915 Civil War Reunion in Richmond per *civilwarcenter.olemiss.edu/reunions.html#* – with the exact date and place.

Well, my father Henry Campbell Slack, 1909-1987, grew up in New York. My mother Mariamne Jenifer Houston Slack, 1913-1964, grew up in Richmond and New York. My grandmother Elizabeth Price Houston, 1882-1949, never lost her southern accent. My mother's lifelong best friend was Roberta Love Tayloe of Powhatan Plantation just west of Williamsburg. I knew Elizabeth as Grandma and have a small-person vision of sitting in her lap and leaning back into comfort while she darned a sock or sewed up a tear. My mother visited Roberta at Powhatan in childhood, and in reverse her family lived with us up North for a time in World War II when husbands were away.

The UCV medal is likely, I now believe, something of my mother's that my father kept among his dearest belongings. Perhaps once in a small brown velvet box with shirt studs and an inherited gold watch.

So I ask the unanswerable. Family papers will show who fought on what side in the Civil War and where, in that awful time. Who attended the UCV reunion in 1915? My mother was merely two at the time and her mother thirty-three. Did Mariamne treasure the medal with memories from her mother or perhaps her best friend? I will need to read the letters and explore the cardboard box and check dates in some family papers handed down, before I have even a chance to know. For now the medal is back in its place beside my chair.

I am not alone in my "if only" thoughts. Pretty much everyone wishes to have asked those last few questions. My siblings are both gone now, so there is no one with whom I can share or confirm this moment's partial revelations.

But I do have the comfort of my own sleuth-work. Perhaps our children will enjoy learning more of the medal's small story. Perhaps our grandchildren . . .

All I know today is that the medal feels like fond history in my hands. And the thought that my father Henry kept it near always, perhaps taking comfort in its reminiscence of my mother Mariamne, gives comfort to me now, today, and for my own forever. ❖

Leaf Blowers

There are two kinds of leaf blowers,
One the swirly invisible wind, and playful –
Maple leaves falling to ground
From high home branches
Soft to the touch in the first hours
Then in days red-gold colorful
Then drying, curling upward
Trending to crisp and tan
Crunchy underfoot, ready for rakes.
Then there is the other leaf blower –
Loud desecrator of morning
In whiny on-again-off-again
Scales of sound, and unwelcoming.
I bless the wind kind.

Sound

Near-silent sound – with window closed
I cannot hear it. Open again, there it is,
The owl, perch hidden in palms,
Later, it is the raucous caws of crows arguing:
"My worm!" "My branch!"

Grandmother

As a grandmother
Of five, all young
I like receiving notes
With backward letters.

Noah and Andrew

Noah and Andrew, two boys ruddy-cheeked,
October rakes briskly at the ready, offered.
Two elders of eighty, grateful, said Yes.
Modest fee settled, red-gold carpet of maple leaves
Drawn exuberantly into leaf heaps and lawn bags.
Day's work well done with laughter and thanks.

Next day, windy beginning, Hello again from the boys.
More leaves down, We'll rake them up for free.
Elders of eighty – Yes, please not for free.
Noah and Andrew – No, it's alright, really.
Red-gold gathered all over again, with joy again
Quiet pride, young-boy smiles, here is grace.

Sand

Sometimes,
Dread comes mid-night
In tosses and turns and wavery fear,
Seeping into troubled dreams,
Jarring me to wakefulness.
Endurance? The future?
The mere tomorrow?
This sickness and health
Stage of things tests the vow.
Where is the joy
Of memory or anticipation?

Yet dread comes
Rarely, fleetingly
And every morning it is
Vanquished. By light.
By hope. By smile, book,
Snowflake, the first flower
By the gift
Given me for life: Blake's
Gift of finding heaven
In a grain of sand.
I understand this now.

Some Things Matthew Doesn't Know

When my first child was born and placed on my breast, I lay there in wonderment. Me? A mother? Oh, how lovely, how lovely. ✳ *When my first grandchild was born, his mother had her own new-mother thoughts, perhaps similar to mine. The gift to me was to care for that grandchild for eight Mondays in Manhattan while his mother, a teacher, completed the school year with her beloved Second Grade students.* ✳ *My joy in this trusting task had nowhere to go but into my journal. This extract from a small unpublished book,* Letters to Matthew, *conveys my sense, again of wonderment, in being a grandmother for the first time. A grandmother! Today I am a grandmother of five. Matthew turned 15 in 2022.*

Matthew Henry Walton, my almost 2-day-old grandson, does not know many things that I know. And I suspect I have lost knowledge of some of the same things he senses in his first hours of life out in the world. Among the things Matthew Henry Walton does not yet know are:

* The look of sunrise the other day, faint hint at first, then fiery pink clouds, low and rising, against illuminated blue sky full of glory.
* The limitless sadness and hopelessness that infuse every moment of many lives, whether from illness, poverty, hunger, war, or absence of love.
* The enormity of the joy in his own weary parents' hearts as they begin day two of fatherhood and motherhood.
* The thanks in a grown-up's heart when a newborn face lights up in recognition.

And in a larger world, Matthew Henry Walton does not yet know about:

* The miracles of a seedling sprouting, of the quiet of summer, the bold colors of our East Coast autumn, the dance of a season's first snowflakes.
* The nourishment of a kind word received or given, or the ache of hurt of unkindness when something else was wished for.
* The reassurance of a sense of belonging, and of the smile of a true friend.
* The profound gratefulness in this grandmother's heart for a blessing received on Day 2 of his life, or to be received on Day 9 in her church, with a flower on the altar and his name Matthew Henry Walton read out in celebration and in honor of miracle.
* The brilliance of design in a tadpole becoming a frog, or a thin line of ants trailing from one place to another, carrying heavy burdens sometimes, and always being purposeful.
* A caring glance, and a blanket, when he is cold.
* Delight in making snow angels.
* The quiet of snow falling all around, and of being the first out in the morning, rabbit footprints the only ones already there. ❖

Out East

From an old Adirondack chair
On an Amagansett roof top,
At hint of sunrise out east
I see pink orange horizon at left,
Low misty clouds soft grey
Along the horizon's adjacent arcs.
Palest gentlest blue sky connects all
In a single lucent dome.

Sound - ocean's steady mere murmur,
Then silence. Why? How on earth?
Perhaps it is the wind at my rooftop
Taking sound away out to sea.
Yes, here it is again, the ocean murmur.
Sound – still crickets or peepers,
No birdsong, not the territory of
First light wren or robin.

Now I see a lone gull purely soaring.
Is he the first of his family awake?
Or perhaps tides are too high just now,
To lay bare the shells, the delicacies
That seagulls prefer, swoop down fast for.
Wind is soft, plays with my hair.
This is serenity. My time of joy,
Silent, deeply beautiful, inspiring,
Reminding of eternal matters.

Sailing in Her Basket Boat

Kierkegaard. Yes, deeply true – best to live life forward and understand it looking back. At eighty at last I see the wisdom of this counsel. Insights do come my way because of it – even in the form of a memoir for my grand-children, so each of the five will know me when they are older and I am gone.

But just now I refer not to understanding a long life gladly if quirkily lived – my own. Instead I am merely going inside for an exploratory look around, recognizing moments held in deepest memory but without order or context or perhaps even meaning.

Some such scenes stay forever, for me. Recorded in memory's theater of the mind, as if from last night or this morning. Flash-frozen from my own olden days or moments ago.

First to mind is a fire. A grand, hot fire in the night, a big old house across the street engulfed, our whole family and all the neighbors gathered to watch. I felt the heat on my face – about six or so I was. Thus more than seventy years past. But I can still see the flames house-high and roaring into black sky, not really frightening to me because I held my mother's hand – but thrilling in heat and enormity. Perhaps a spark from a vagrant, they said the next day – suburban house empty between owners. Nobody really knew. It was just past the early 1940s wartime, and blackout curtains and lots else were happening.

Of a younger night I can still see two glowing eyes in the dark of my bedroom, I as usual sent resentfully upstairs first as the youngest child. At that moment my bare foot touched something shaggy – a monster! It was terrifying and I leapt up and I needed my mother's arms of comfort and reassurance – "It was just the cat . . . It was just the cat." I was scared of the dark for some while after. I can still see the glowing eyes in my black-dark room, and picture – as I could see in the morning – the furry, scratchy twine hanging down from door handle to floor. The villain twine? Likely left over from games the day before.

Talk of memories! Everyone old enough today remembers where he was when man first walked on the moon. I was upstairs at my sister's in Connecticut, and she wakened her daughter to come see it happening and know that she had done so. My memory still sees the black and white television with its old-shaped screen, and Neil Armstrong lumbering along the moon's craggy surface.

Likewise for Kennedy's assassination – I was on a West 28th Street sidewalk in Manhattan's flower district, enjoying lunchtime sunlight near work at a horticulture magazine. Freddy Rivera, long a trusted messenger for our magazine, told me the news. Young and slender Freddy, black haired, handsome, freckles – he told me and we both cried. Hugs helped us right then and there. I can still clearly see Freddy, his dark shiny hair, his tears, the sidewalk we stood on. The pain is gone. The vivid picture is still here.

And the same for 9/11 – how did you hear? Where were you? Life turned into awfulness that day – we were all taken by surprise. And in the changed clime following we remember strings of stunningly terrible images, brought live as tragedy happened. School shootings, pandemic death, Capitol riot, heedless massacre. Unthinkable daily news.

So today I need offsetting treasure-memories, lest I sink into the chasm of awful; the TV-internet-press reporters thrive on bad. My emblazoned memories need a lift.

So I remember instead, palliatively, my son's face as he stood at the altar looking past me down-aisle to his almost bride – his look expectant, nervous, proud, handsome, sweet. I can see his look precisely all these years later. His loyalty, appropriately, leaving mother for wife and children of his own.

And I can hear the womanly moan that came from my daughter, and see her as she neared the birth of her second daughter. On her side, her husband near, that moment I remember myself when the pain is such that you say, "I will never go through this again." Now my daughter has two girls to grow up with their counterpart three boy cousins.

I was with this newest little girl on her first birthday, parents and

 older sister soon to be home from work and school. She climbed into a little woven toy-basket on the floor, sitting upright and glancing over at me, so proud of being there, and wearing a knitted pink hat. Perhaps she was out sailing in her basket boat. I can see her there. She is older now, seven at least, and reading herself to sleep. But the image of the proud wearer of the pink hat sitting upright in her basket is mine forever.

Why do these memories of all sorts and sizes go into that special forever file drawer in our memories? There's no chronological order, no category of daze or fear, no "file here" instruction from me. They just go to the deepest or dearest place, available upon request or if triggered somehow.

It is a mystery to me, this emblazoned level of recollection. Today I go searching around for my cellphone, and I do know to put my keys on the hook by the front door and my credit card back in my wallet immediately. Elder memory is iffy. Which is fine. Yet how do those searing or endearing memories get to that deepest place? ❖

Bathing

Yesterday, a dozen sparrow-size birds
jostled and flapped as they bathed
in a puddle across the street.
It was early morning's sweet sort of calm
so the antics of each appeared twice,
in reflection. The puddle was
ten-inch slender yet ran the full width
of a driveway's old concrete apron –
a bluestone and black tar connection.
Nothing fancy, but bird-perfect.
Droplets from their wings caught light.
Twitters and tiny splashing sounds
crossed the street to me.
I watched the frolic, a bystander by chance,
silent on my own front porch.

Betrayal Is a Big Word!

I fail at betrayal, whether real or imagined, recent or remembered, by me or of me.

Betrayal is a big word. Needs capitalization and italics – *Betrayal*! Plots of plays and books are built around it. Romantic entanglements get more entangled because of it. It's such a big word that it seems too big for my long mostly happy life. But if you take away its weighty "betrayal of trust" sense, and settle the word down to something more ordinary, I guess there have been times where people didn't play fair with me, or perhaps I didn't play so fair myself.

First forth are twin firings at beloved museums, now thirty-five and twenty-five or so years ago. However, to be betrayed, don't you need a trust that gets betrayed? In the first firing, the Director-firer wept and I had to comfort him; not enough money to afford me . . . staff cuts . . . so sad, at the place I had worked for sixteen years and helped to found, where everyone said "You're the soul of the place. They could never fire *you*!" Yes I trusted this man, but dire financial straits meant laying off all vice presidents in one day. That meant me. That's life. I called some friends and we all went out for beers.

Two weeks later, my last day, "Come back in a year and we'll consider rehiring or severance after your sixteen years of service," another executive said.

A year later he said merely, "Well, we considered it."

Guess that counts as betrayal, now that I mention it. What a rat. Never had trusted him, though. He lived in *Upper* Brookville, hid his handsome pale Black skin as tan, wore slender-legged ever-so suits – and, rumor has it, charged his rental cars to the dire-straits museum.

The other firing really doesn't count: the firer was simply wicked. I'd been at that museum for nine years, he just one, and I never liked or trusted him. No trust, no betrayal. New doors opened soon.

Then there was the local beach club chillout when I declined to take sides in an acrimonious divorce. I liked both halves of the bitterness. We had invited the two halves to a cocktail party, telling each of the invitation to the other. He soon married anew and we four were friends till his death years later in Santa Fe; he lies peacefully in the ground under a tree. But She had friends who loved me one minute and went to silent stares the day after cocktails. I can still see the Club wives aligned in the sand towel beside towel, looking up as I went by; no glimmer, nothing. Invisible me.

That got resolved when I wrote a love letter to the Her and said let's do better, and we did. The Club wives did relax. But oh, those parallel towels and those frigid looks.

Kind of boring betrayal-wise thus far, isn't it?

I do remember a birthday party to which my sixth-grade public-school daughter was not invited. "We had to draw the line somewhere," said the private school mother. Of course my daughter learned of the *private* private-school party when her friends at the beach melted away one by one on a Wednesday afternoon. Not sure who hurt more at that, this mother or her uninvited daughter. Daughter forgave. I took time. Where does all that fit on the Betrayal spectrum?

The quintessential quasi-betrayal was not of me but by me and long ago. Growing up in scenic New Jersey, where no one told me not to bring a Jewish friend or a Black friend home because there were none, I met Margaret in fourth grade or so. We would roller-skate to school together, and with my own zero sense of self-worth she was my faithful friend. I can still see her soft amiable face and perhaps she is a retired CEO today, with her gentle wise ways. But what I do remember, forever, is my mother's remark that I should not bring Margaret home because she was "common."

Never today would my mother say such a thing, but the Social Register gave people bad old ideas, and she died fifty years ago before she could outgrow such concepts. To understate, I never grew into them, with regret that they ever existed in my life and times.

The betrayal? I wince to ask. Did I stay friends with Margaret?

I do not remember, and hope seventy years later that I did. Wish I could recall a defiant "I'm bringing Margaret home and I don't care what you say!"

But I was still obedient daughter setting the table and making my bed as requested. So I'll never know about the betrayal or not of my friend Margaret. ❖

Found in October

By now I have lost morning runs
among golden maples, mother father
brother sister friends gone –
and many strengths of my youth,
My innocent easy youth.
By now I know truly of lies and losses
And fearsome fires and floods.
Each day tells me more.
Each day hurts my heart, my hope.

Yet I find joy in the smallest things,
more precious in light of such
sad surrounds, and new understanding
in wisdoms come down through time.
And I see the smile of a fellow
lonely elder in the supermarket,
a stranger, glad for my notice
of her elegantly long grey-pink-white
sweater: "My son-in-law gave this to me."

And I see the innocent eyes
of a gold-winged princess
on our doorstep, saying Thank You
as mother-instructed
for her choice of Halloween candy
from the dear old salad bowl
held forward in my hand.
Oh, in this world of losses and findings
So much has come my way.

Chores

The mere word sounds heavy-laden,
Bothersome. Fold sheets / take out the trash
Vacuum-dust / empty-fill the dishwasher / pay bills
Clean the kitchen sink / call the plumber to fix
The leak. Even the chore verbs are a bore –
Pay-fold-change-empty-dust-call. Where is
The poetry in these tedious terms?

This morning, folding soft clean sheets
Unhurriedly, I thought of shelter cots,
Fifth-day clothes, uncertainty, sparse suppers
Shortened shopping lists, triaging the bills.
My morning chore – folding clean sheets and shirts
while coffee brews – is newly seen as sacred.
Household tasks are my own fortune's smile.

Winds and Silences

Summer – Nature is pruning her trees today.
On a windy walk on a late-July morning I see
pine cones down, green oak leaves and early acorns,
a fiesta surprise for squirrels and they know it.

Fall – In my yard, today, frondy hemlock arms
wave in the breeze of morning. Tenacious vines
atop a tall wind-broken spruce turn red-gold.
Dogwood backlit in early sun is radiant, red-brown.
Silence wins, other than chittery squirrel or perhaps cicada
and for sure now a crow. It is the season for slanty sun.
Acorns come down in tiny crashes, in rustly wind.

Winter – Morning quietness. Out for a walk,
I find such silence and stillness it's as if
something big happened in the world and
I'm the only one who doesn't know about it.

Spring – Morning breeze – Look at the maple tops
laughing and dancing irresponsibly, each branch
freshly dressed to the nines and heading for sky.
Everything is beginning again.

Lexicon

First snow fell
Today, in almost 2020
Reminding me
Age almost 80 . . .
Ice Man
Fuller Brush Man
Milk Man
Knife Sharpener Man
Ice Box
Juke Box
Victory Garden
Roller Skate to School.
One day
I will define each
For our grandies
As they someday
May do for their own:
"Years ago, when
I was a child . . . "

Maples in Autumn

It is Halloween, almost.
Oh dear. May the hint
Of Nor'easter wind merely
Rustle the front yard maples,
Fiery orange again,
First leaves strewn below
In a glorious pink-tinged carpet.
May the wind be mild, to keep
Wavy sunny branches
Half-full at least,
Still resplendent,
Awaiting the goblins
And princesses
And guiding parents
Who always come
And comment –
Maple tree blessings.

Summertime Visits
In My Neighborhood

*"When you walk along a country road
and notice a little tuft of grass,
the next time you pass that way you must stop
to see how it is getting along and how much it has grown."*
- GEORGIA O'KEEFFE

In kinship with Georgia O'Keeffe, I stopped to visit some familiar creations today. Their well-beings, and all the other growing things I see, always touch my morning walk. Each has its own history as one of God's projects, from seed stage to flourishing springs and summers. Each finds its way in life miraculously, innocent of the world's ills. My creations list does not include the luxuriant weeds whose names I do not know, but I do see them and admire their complexities and lusty boldness.

Among this morning's summertime visits in my neighborhood –

* The lilies of the valley around the corner, a shaded swath along an old split-rail fence. Each was nestled white in green two weeks ago, and each time I pass by I intend to ask the owner if I can pick some stems for a little vase at home. I have never asked him. But the swath remains reminiscent of the beds of lilies of the valley of my childhood home in New Jersey. The tiny white bells around the corner are spent now, but I will watch for them again next year.

* The hot pink rhododendron. It is botanical-gardenesque and lives on a lawn edge just a block or two from my house. A week ago it was festooned in gorgeous pink blossoms. Its profusion made you marvel at one plant creating and maintaining such an array. Like an orchestra with exquisite strength and timing for a symphony of shoot, bud, and blossom. Yesterday all was still resplendent. Fading will come well before Solstice, yes, but next year that beautiful dress of pink blossoms will be back I am sure.

* Oh, and the forsythia! Of course the classic yellow is long gone because forsythia is so angelic to come so soon after the weeks of ice and darkness. But once the yellow bracts gave way to green, the newest shoots lengthened to curve out and up, striving toward the sun. These naked new branch extensions just thrived there quietly for a while. But almost overnight they came covered in their own first green, all arching skyward in this their freshman summer. Today these newest leaves open in vees pointing straight up, like the mouths of baby birds. Next year they can join all their fellow branchlets in that yellow that heralds winter's completion. And by summer they will relax into the gentle green downward arc of seasoned branches.

* The baby maples further along and around another corner, back toward my house. Wow. They came to the neighborhood last October, three staked spindly trees with just a few broken brown leaves just hanging on. I worried for these trees – not braced for our wintry winds. Come April I walked by and stood up close. The branches were worrisomely sparse, with buds timid and very far apart. So I thought oh goodness this tree is not a happy tree. Its buds are way far apart . . . I guess that's all it can manage.

Well, now I know to honor the sparseness. Each bud swelled and swelled into the most enormous russet red leaf: dark, lush, and almost a hand-width wide, perfectly spaced in nature's intention. Soon each of the three young ones wore a dense, glistening cluster of leaves. Then the clusters loosened, relaxing outward, each perfect leaf now free to rustle in the wind. What a fine showing for its first summer in our neighborhood.

* And then there is the geranium sprout in my sunroom. A year ago I cut off all but an inch from all stems in this plant. It was old and leggy in its terra cotta pot and would grow back stronger, was the idea. Not so. All that happened was four tan inch-tall stalks doing nothing. Then came one tiny green extrusion from one desiccated stem. The tiny tip grew in miniscule amounts, hardly discernible day to day. So did a competing weed that appeared next to it from the old pot's life outdoors. The weed outstripped the sprout and goodbye. But the sprout grew and thickened and now is a proud new geranium plant all on its own. I do believe I see a hint of a blossom to be. ❖

Twice Shy

Madeline, thank you.

You showed me the peril of knowing too much about an author. Twenty years or so ago – or was it thirty? – my dream of hearing you speak came to be. It was uptown at the Cathedral of St John the Divine, such a beautiful place. Madeline L'Engle, creator of *A Wrinkle in Time*, the story of a tesseract, a magic moment in time where no time elapsed. Where Mrs Who, a mythical furry creature who had no eyes but conveyed love and comforted children, said to them, "You do not need eyes to see, to love." Oh, the thought of meeting you, Madeline!

But it was awful. Your words, your manner, all those Cathedral minutes were not magical. You were old enough to be successful, to "know your worth," to seem jaundiced and far from the gentle stuff of your books. Looking back, I see only now that you taught me to read the book, love the book, and stay away from the author's life and actual way of being. But I forgot all that.

So when a friend suggested I write of a favorite author or artist, I went to Google for Frost (no; endless analysis), for Millay (no; bisexual open marriage; fine but TMI, didn't need to know that), for Dickenson (no; reclusive, her young self dwelt overly on death), and – the killer – for my honored Martin Buber, whose *I and Thou* entered my soul long ago with beautiful wisdoms (no; "Buber in 12 Minutes," a video).

Horrors.

Buber had carried me through the confusions of college years and all years since – the dance between minds, the comfort of souls connecting, or not.

I remember the kindness of the professor who introduced Buber and me.

So now I further forbore to look into Lamott, Lindbergh, Gould, Potter, E. B. White – anyone who had lit up my life with words. Betty Smith wrote *A Tree Grows in Brooklyn* – I just finished it and loved it and desire to know nothing of her life beyond what her words suggest. Just before that it was *The Good Earth* – Pearl Buck's classic, powerful recounting of impoverished times in China. I'll stay away from her bio. And then I read the enchanting story for children *The One and Only Ivan*. Katherine Applegate wrote it in recent years and my grandson loved it. I know nothing about the author. Perfect! My recognition is this: for me, keep the intermediaries away. Let me read Robert Frost and be touched. Anne Lamott too. All of them. Just fine on my own, perhaps less "understanding" than a 12-minute video or scholar's interpretation might be. But that's fine. More than fine. In the movie *Shadowlands*, I remember, C. S. Lewis asked his students: "Why do we read?"

Glib answers came from all except one student. Lewis asked him relentlessly "Why do we read?" and failed again and again to elicit an answer.

Then one day the answer came: "We read to know we are not alone." Wow. That is why we read. That is why I read. That is why the son of my college roommate took a book to church with him for his mother's too early funeral service thirty years ago.

There is safety in books. Comfort. An I-Thou connection between reader and author: "I understand! I feel that way too. I am not alone in my despair, my joy, my doubt, my love."

So, Madeline, thank you for the lesson I learned, forgot, and, twice shy, learned again: skip the intrusive truths of the author's life. It's just the author's words and me. ❖

Rest

I am desperate to rest,
Devoid of verve, energy, any sense
Of succeeding in my intentions.
I am sad, weary, disinterested.
Love letters, the next book, plants
(unflowering in neglect) –
Everything eludes me.
Therefore,
I will turn to the smallest joys
In all that is at hand. Walks
Friends, books, helping, offering
Giving, serving, savoring
Perhaps even daring new things.

As Old as December

Lee Rushmore was no more than eighty-five when we met. Close to my own age today. I was fifty or so, fresh in the empty nest era of motherhood. Lee was as old as December, our friendship as new as May.

We worked together at a Quaker elementary school in Westbury, Long Island, Lee and I: he as venerable board member and volunteer, I as development staff. Our friendship turned to love over time, I believe – love that lends strength to the task at hand, love that warms the day upon reflection.

Lee was hardly handsome. He was a tall gentleman, bald, ample of girth, and jowly with time. He stuttered oftentimes; I learned not to complete his sentences. He was also winsome – a well-dressed Quaker elder, long retired from corporate life, with sharp-witted wife and successful children.

Our tasks were to build five classrooms, and then a library, for the children of all colorful sorts who were swelling the student ranks: Black, White, Asian, Hispanic, mixed race. Single parent, guardian grandmother, mixed heritage parents. Adopted or not, confident or not, modestly disabled or not. All children age four to twelve would learn in the classrooms and borrow books in the library we sought to build. A rainbow of readers and learners.

We daydreamed our plans, Lee and I. He then crafted our daydreams, handwritten, in precise round-lettered memos. I ordered and formalized the memos into proposals, and together we persuaded foundations and civic-spirited individuals to fund our projects. Lee invited gifts by generous example. We felt ourselves a formidable team.

Every encounter with Lee was cheering and productive. Oftentimes our talk drifted to the personal – our own children and dreams, the school's challenges in management and clashing personalities, the aims and shortfalls of the Quaker Meeting House "meeting for worship" tradition. For instance, how to blend modern behaviors with the scuffed brown wooden benches, the intimidating "facing bench" from which Meeting was led, the twin doorways that had kept the sexes separate two hundred years ago? Lee understood both worlds and offered amiable solutions.

Somewhere along the way Lee found cemetery records to confirm what I came to suspect, hearing all those old Quaker names. Yes, he discovered, my father's many-greats grandparents had married in the Westbury Meeting House in 1795. Whitehead Hicks and Margaret Titus. Lee and I decided it would be lovely to be cousins. Distant and dear.

One day I brought in some words I had found in a new Quaker leaflet. The words were the favorite, self-empowering prayer of a late Member of Meeting: Lord, what can I do differently today? Lee had brought in the very same prayer to me. It has guided my life since that day.

I came to realize Lee and I were antidotes for the missing pieces of each other's lives. My parents and grandparents were early gone and my marriage, like Lee's, long and good and settled. Our tasks gave him enlivening purpose in decades of retirement, and perhaps a respite from the quiescence of family life. For me, ours was friendly work in an office often hostile to my privileged life, and in a too-quiet empty nest at home. Our classrooms and library came beautifully into being – bright colors, modern shelving and desks, walls adorned with alphabets and dancing numbers. Seeing children and teachers love them warmed the hearts of us all.

At one point illness arrived for Lee. Pain came, walking required a cane and then a walker as balance lost out to even greater weakness. He voiced no complaint, showed no fear. One day, as if anticipating our parting, Lee brought me a painting he had given his wife many years ago; no room in their smaller house now. It was cactus in flower in a quiet, faded desert scene. I was just home from rapturous spring with my friend Lucy in Arizona. Home from fields of yellow poppies and purple lupine, whole canyons of wild color in which Lucy and I hiked and painted and wrote things nestled against rocks out of sight of each other, lost in the morning. Lee loved my telling of this, and his gift reflected our two differing but resplendent desert times.

Lee died at ninety-one after a brief hospital stay, fondly regarded by friends of many kinds Quaker and otherwise. I hope my cheery notes reached him, and that he thought back to the affection and wicked hilarity in our worthy work. I will forever honor his lessons of persuasion, daring, and faith. ❖

Spirit

Yesterday I forgot
To be grateful.
Forgot the world's ills.
I lazed, saddened,
Mulled over my own
Wrongs and losses.
Stayed indoors
On the sunniest day.
Felt equal to nothing.

Today light rain makes
Tiny sounds outside.
Morning is lightest grey.
I yearn for a walk
And will take it.
Sadness seems gone
In hope for the world.
Life is playing
With my spirit.

Living With Richard and Emeline

Emeline…I imagine long swirling ecru taffeta gown with seed-pearl bodice, hair swept up in combs, pearls at the neck. I have Emeline's sterling silver baby cup – intricately engraved in flowing script, tarnishing away on my living room shelf until I buff it into proper silvery brilliance. I do this only every now and then.

Emeline Furman Coe – Emeline for elegance as I've imagined, Coe for an old family name I know well. And Furman – as I long believed – for her happy (surely happy!) marriage to Gabriel Furman Coe, the namesake of Brooklyn's pier street paralleling the water, just south of the Brooklyn Bridge. How influential Emeline and Gabriel must have been! A harbor-edge street was named for them! How opportune that I, a descendent, once lived four stories up along that very street in Brooklyn. I overlooked the selfsame harbor. I saw ships dock at the Furman Street piers, and even wrote stories about freighters and tugs busy at work beside my namesake street.

And then there is Richard Lee Campbell – an ancestor of unexplored connection, whose silver and cut-crystal Tiffany flask sits near Emeline's cup on the living room shelf. The flask endures the same polish-tarnish-polish cycle of neglect as Emeline's cup. I love its light-catching linear facets, its elegant monogram RLC all curlicued and intertwined. What a dashing man he must have been, whoever he was. Family legend has it that Richard Lee Campbell – my father Henry's middle name was Campbell, and beyond that I haven't worked out the connection – was lost at sea. Was Richard related to statesman Richard Henry Lee of Declaration of Independence fame? How exactly was he connected to my father of the shared Campbell name? Why was he out at sea – as a naval officer, perhaps in a Famous Maritime Conflict?

Enter online searching, a digital knight on white charger, carrying answers. I had checked Emeline just for fun for a memoir I wrote for our children. (In the book's "Midland Street House Tour" addendum I say, for instance, "This was ancient Aunt Marguerite's mahogany slant-top desk – we used to visit her for Thanksgiving with Upper East Side lace tablecloths and crystal finger bowls; I longed to clink a spoon against mine as if calling the table to order." And the addendum mentions Emeline's cup and Richard's flask, which drifted down to me amidst other family things. I had asked no questions at the time – blind me – and their stories went silently on to heaven with my parents.)

Now for the digital enlightenment. Emeline is spelled with an e, not an a, as I had first thought. She was born in 1853 and married at age twenty-nine not to the mythical Gabriel Furman Coe – whose actual name was merely Gabriel Furman – but to . . . the Richard Lee Campbell of the flask!

One fantasy shatters and others take form. Gabriel Furman was an outstanding nineteenth-century Brooklyn citizen of many sorts, until he died in his fifties, they say, from opium and penury. The Furman Street railway ran north along water's edge from Cobble Hill to Fulton Ferry, carrying passengers to and from the East River ferry slips. Rail freight barges crisscrossed the river with goods for New Jersey and the ocean-traveling ships at the piers. Gabriel Furman is no relation to me whatsoever. That's too bad; my maritime origins myth is still intact through other predecessors, but a long-held chunk of it just fell away.

And now I am left not knowing. If Richard Lee Campbell was lost at sea, when did it happen? What was life like for Emeline and Richard in New York of the 1850s? Should I move them together from their perches – near each other but not lovingly adjacent – on my living room shelf?

All surmises are still surmises, regarding Richard and Emeline, other than their marriage when she was twenty-nine. Who knows if she wore swirly taffeta or he fought bravely at sea? But for now, living with Richard and Emeline as I have for my lifetime, secrets stay as I pass by her silver cup and his cut-crystal flask. As if cup and flask would tell me stories if only they could. Perhaps Google – such a guttural sound against the softness of Emeline – will someday tell me more. ❖

Tiny Girl

Tiny girl all innocence
blond, beautiful unknowingly
presents her grandfather
with bright crayoned art –
flag, turkey, heart, love words
hand lettered in capitals,
large, slanting off-page.
Bashful tiny girl
heart-grateful grandfather
Thanksgiving.

Mr Robinson's Silver

Our first fight before marriage fifty-seven years ago was about Mr Robinson. His silver. The markings on the back of a spoon or fork. Should we choose the letter W for the fiancé's last name? Or "properly" the letter S for the bride-to-be's maiden name, as was still the dowry tradition of the day. Fiancé Walton won. So Mr Robinson's silver – the noted James Robinson Silversmiths Inc. – received, along with its four esteemed hallmarks, a tiny (handsome) W on each of its Queen Anne forks and spoons. Knives in the Robinson "octagonal pistol handle" style cannot appropriately take a marking. So be it! The wedding took place.

All this makes me look back today. Who on earth was the then-famed James Robinson? Why do my daughter and seemingly all daughters scorn silverware vs stainless steel "flatware"? (Awful term.) Why are these tried-and-true traditions swept away these days?

The answer lies in "tried and true" and "these days."

Mr Robinson first. I never thought about it, when my almost-husband Bob and I went to James Robinson Silversmiths Inc., impressive in the East Fifties near Fifth, more than a half century ago. Were we buzzed in? Was it still that kind of place? Tradition flourished there sufficiently that I never questioned a thing. This was our chosen pattern: Queen Anne. Family friends could give us place settings: perfect. Yes it was costly but that's all part of it ($80 for a twelve-piece place setting then, $209 for one knife today; rumor has it a full place setting replacement now $22,000.)

Then blissfully onward to the plates – Wedgewood Wildflower for every day, blue-and-gold-rimmed Cornflower Limoges for dinner parties. Next Baccarat wine, water, cordial, and champagne for the crystal. That's just the way it was done forever ago. I didn't think twice amidst the flurry of it all.

James Robinson, I search to discover only now fifty some years later, must have been pretty impressive. In silversmithing skills, in sartorial appearance, in Upper Mid-Town aura. Nowhere in my brief googlings, however, can I find his background and whether he affected the starched collar and trim black and grey-tipped beard that I imagined. Did he have children? A happy life? It's like searches for my ancestors – I can find names and dates but no characteristics – what were their lives like? Their loves and tasks and foibles?

I find only that my Mr Robinson bought the late Englishman Bertram Fletcher Robinson's silversmith firm in 1912 – with its Master Craftsman lineage dating back to the 1550s – so that the art of hand-forged flatware could flourish across the ocean in New York. Fletcher Robinson's "The Story of a Living Craft" (engaging video at *jrobinson.com*) documents the skills that create a hand-forged silver spoon – from slender silver bar to annealing to hand hammering to shaping to polishing in all the nooks and crannies of silver fork tines – intricate lengthy beautiful stuff. I love our silverware, jumbled together in Pacific-clothed drawer and experienced in dishwashering. I held one of our spoons with new reverence after seeing that documentary.

James Robinson died two decades after his 1912 purchase, and his brother-in-law Edward Munves succeeded him. It was Edward Munves, I remember the man and the quiet elegant place, who sold us our silver in 1965.

Oh my, times have changed. Who thinks about Mr Robinson today? Or the intricacies of his silversmithing craft? Who even wants silver today – you'd have to polish it.

The silver spoon metaphor as luxury of birth, as foolish excess – and the lengthy silversmithing process itself – exemplify the "tried and true" (read old-fashioned, out-of-date, no time for it) ways of doing things. It is all so Yesterday. New less costly tastes now, move on.

But how would poor Mr Robinson feel about today? Old reverences gone in favor of new ones – computers, computer games, websites, cellphones, the black pits and time-wasters and splendors and threats of the internet? What happened to civil discourse and unhurried conversations and sitting and listening to the radio? His head would spin. His heart would stop.

And it gets worse . . . nobody wants that "brown furniture" anymore today – the kind with brasses agleam in the Metropolitan, the inherited mahogany treasures so lovingly polished by generations. They have been eclipsed by new reverence for sectional sofas and open concept kitchens. And what about the leisurely Sunday dinners with children asking why the sky is blue, and conversation taking its time? Commuter trains and the whole pace of life are culprits in the loss of the family dinner custom. Oh my, I exhibit my senior-generation membership with observations like these.

I do not long for the old days! I love my cellphone and all it derives from and all it permits. I cherish a gallimaufry of things and thoughts, all vintages and sizes. I thank goodness for medicines and neighborhood friends and kind moments in our lives. And a million other gifts of a million kinds.

But I so admire the care, the lavishing of attention and skills upon the James Robinson silver spoon in my hand, marked with a W for us a lifetime ago. And I still take pleasure remembering the whole old-fashioned ceremonial selection of our silver, china, and crystal. Who will savor them, or see them as silly, when we are gone off to play mahjong in the sky? ❖

Common Cold

Taken ill
I ache
It is not cancer
It is not bombs
Not a child hurt
It is hot eyeballs
Sneezes
Snuffly nose
Wretched sinus
Pressuring me
It is frog voice
Scratchy throat
I am not even
Crotchety
Who cares?
Nothing is possible
Not one thing.
Perhaps someday
A glimmer of
Otherwise?

St. John's Church

White steepled sanctuary
Same seat or near it
Same people known or not
Same light from one window
Blue green silver white
Same comfort, longing
Same sadness, hope
Same sense of belonging
Same sermon sound
Singing sound quietness
Love surrounding
Sunday after Sunday.

Love

I am happy
He is essential
We are grateful
This is our own old love.

No One

January 23, 2020
Today is my father's birthday
There is no one to tell
Not my mother
Not my brother
Not my sister
Nor his own
Who would care?
Perhaps some up yonder.
There, he is 111 today
Or perhaps only 78
His age when he died
When I held his hand
And said it's okay Daddy
Do they keep count
Up in heaven?

Beautiful Tree

I am like a beautiful tree –
weathered, gnarly a little
reflecting health and wealth
of sun, water, love, resilience
ready for my seasons.

Vermeer

Vermeer woman
Stocky girth, aproned
Pouring the morning's milk
Pitcher to kitchen's bowl.
She is calm, eyes intent.
No galumphing swoosh of white
From her hands, unhurried
Just a quiet task
Of everyday importance.
My morning tasks
Please me this way too.

Stranger Story Foolishness

Forever ago, my sister Elizabeth and I fooled around with stories. Who is she, we'd wonder out loud, that woman over there? What's the meaning of the red scarf? She's meeting an old high school friend and the scarf is her ID, we'd say. Or actually she hates the color and wears it in penance – she dissed her aging widowed mother the other day and needs time to figure what's next: keep on defiantly or knuckle under to Elder Care? And on and on we'd go in this pass-the-time fantasy foolishness, my sister and I.

In this case the occasion was a drive down the coast to Charleston, South Carolina, a city to explore in our sister-days sans spouses and empty-nest children and Junior League committee commitments. En route we found the shaggy Chincoteague ponies, beloved to me since my childhood reading Marguerite Henry books. We stayed overnight en route on skinny Hatteras Island in a windy storm … heard creepy sounds and admitted they scared us. We toured Charleston with a happenstance guide who was lovely and invited us home for tea at her parents' house edging the Cooper River.

We made up stories about all sorts of strangers we encountered, sisters' minds at play: – the rangers near the ponies, the elegant "ever-so" ladies in the Charleston garden gatherings, the guide herself. I remember Elizabeth's quiet smile when again and again – way back then – I waited for her to lean across and unlock the passenger side door of her snazzy new red car for me. But door locks were newly automatic back then, and I kept forgetting the door was already free. All playful things, these – fixing our memories in time.

So I can certainly tell stories about my sister and my family and my friends, but for the life of me I cannot remember the stranger-stories themselves, from that New York – to – Hatteras – to – Charleston trip.

That occasion was Stranger-Stories 101 for me, my debut and my training for a lifetime of this doodling around with words and imaginings, but it can yield no tales for today.

So, skip thirty years to yesterday. In early morning, I saw a couple walking in my neighborhood. Two blocks away they were, and they turned off to another block and we did not happen to pass each other. Tiny wonderings – perhaps they were at last discussing divorce. Perhaps they were planning to buy an island in the Caribbean, as in HGTV's Island Hunters. Perhaps they had a son newly in college and he kept calling home, homesick but needing to buck up and get a grip: how to handle that? But they never got close enough for my fancy to fly, so they won't do here either. And of course, it matters not a whit. Walks are best for mulling things, planning next steps, resolving concerns, finding peace. Not for idle mental inventions.

Now skip to a pharmacy parking lot some hours later. Next to me – comfortably occupying a slot marked "Messengers only" – was a black car throbbing with loud music that rocked the whole car. Its occupant's elbow rested on the window opening – the better for sound sent blaring to the world's ears. His wife was inside getting medications, I decided. No, it was Halloween candy early – and a costume befitting the stature of their son for the big night. Son and buddies – they had made the Travel Team in soccer too - had plans for the prime neighborhood in town, and the get-up was key....

Well, that partial surmise ended abruptly, because I entered the pharmacy's magic auto-doors and tended to my own errands. Cut! I will never know the truth of Travel Team or Halloween.

So, skip to yesterday afternoon. I drove my walk-challenged husband Bob to the bank – the one with no stairs, so he can hold on to a post and work the

ATM without falling down. It's our new place. I sit in the car and play scrabble on my cellphone, and he and his cane take as long as they need.

Enter a perfect fantasy-story subject: motorcycle man, good healthy rumbly bike sound, grand shiny machine, skillful parking in a non-parking place just tucked in expertly. Over the seat swings the man's leg – hefty fellow, white tee shirt, helmet off now and striding to the bank door.

Inside he goes and waits an eternity for my Bob to thread a check through the ATM, then leans over out of sight, as I learn a minute later, to help him do so.

Motorcycle Man needs a pen. My wife always has one, says Bob. Out comes the man for my pen and we talk. Grey mustache, kindly manner.

"Yes I have a pen. I'm an editor – I always have a pen," I say.

Whereupon we talk – his daughter loves books, loves words, and on we go for a moment – strangers daring to have a small intimate unguarded time. A one-minute meeting of spirits and then off he goes back to the ATM.

Now we are leaving, Bob and I, he back in the car after laborious steps. We pass motorcycle man and he waves and we wave and a bit of grace enters our lives.

Who is this well-along father whose daughter reads too many books? Who stops to help my Bob? Who sports a hefty belly and rides a cool-ass bike with clear pleasure? There's a story there...

I imagine that he has a son too, just out of college so the bike celebrates the end of tuition payments. His daughter hides in books just as I do (and just as I did sixty years ago) – this last he told me. I feel kinship with this book-shy daughter I'll never meet.

On and on I could go in my surmising – Motorcycle Man is happily married but Wife wants him to lose weight. He loves the bike and She worries.

(He is – and I do remember this offhand comment of his – an engineer.) He likes his job but the weekend biking is the freeing thing. He comes to this bank on weekends: it's easy to park the bike there, his favorite deli is nearby, and later he will meet up with two friends who like their bikes too. One of them drives too fast and one day he'll skid and shred leather...

That's it. Silly, the frivolous playing, the making-things-up. It's more fun with a friend anyway, as it was with my sister. I say this and she adds that, and we get gleefully preposterous. Things that I notice she has noticed too and her take way differs from mine. It's a playful thing to do, make up stories on a trip – the fellow in the gas station – what's his life like? The woman in the gift shop in Charleston, silver coifed and attentive – is she a volunteer, or needs the money at this stage? Is she married? Wanted to be? Was but hated it? No end of wondering, and it's all silly really.

And that, in these parlous times, is sacred stuff. ❖

Take Notice

Indoors on this cold, cold
February morning
Each of my hands can feel
The warmth of the other.
In the haste of my days
I had never noticed.
Outside my window
Rhodies curl their leaves
Into spiky clusters,
Tight and down.
Come summer, leaf-fingers
Splay flat, relaxed as lily pads.

Lovely Laundry

Today, asking if death is preferable to how I feel with the flu, I am free from all non-essential things. I feel dreadful. Ache, cough, croaky voice, sinus hammers, extreme fatigue – all are mine. Flowering plants, kitchen napkins, laundry, facial moisturizer – outside my survival space. I care zero for the customary tasks of watering, folding, morning ablutions. Who cares?

In addition, I am free to sleep in my clothes, eat unhealthily all day including chocolate upon demand, and ignore the tax papers waiting on the dining room table. Just as I did with baby toys eons ago before the end-of-day clean-up, so today I walk right by trash baskets, leave the newspaper folded askew, and leave the dog bowls in the middle of the floor.

It is freeing, this feeling-terrible thing. It is in some way like living on a boat with babies: wash clothes only when they visibly need it. Live sparingly. Ponder life in the cockpit at dusk with a tumbler of wine, all cares faraway ashore.

Realistically, my life, most lives, are full of daily obligations and that is fine. But today I can ignore all those. No "have-to's" only "want-to's" and I don't want to do anything. No straightening, arranging, planning, purchasing, laundering for me today. The refrigerator is bare. So it is time for all those frozen things that have been there forever. But later.

In the obligation vacuum, I am free to wander afield. What would I save if the house burned down? My mother's painting of forsythia and pussy willow in a blue and white porcelain vase? I watched her paint it. What were her own feel-dreadful words when she had the flu or its equivalent? Wish we could talk. She died 50 years ago in an earlier world.

Would I save my *Let It Be* poster of marram grass and sand? My little carved wooden St Francis statue, my morning amulet? My Christmas cactus blooming across the room in April in brave confusion? The ruby-pearl-diamond flowers pin I designed with my father?

Would I be happier washing sheets in the Ganges? And far afield it goes, this mental worldly wandering outside the box.

What if I just skipped my late-Christmas-Happy-Spring cards this year? It's already April. Heresy.

What's wrong with just lying around like this? Nothing at all. Nothing whatsoever. I can do it all day long. Tomorrow too. I'll do it.

***

Except a day later, another Today, there is a stirring of possibility. Hours and nights of rest and lazing thoughts have gone by. Yes I can manage to rinse my cereal bowl. Have some more coffee. I traipse to the kitchen for water and I remember the laundry in the dryer from the other day. The day just before flu's decimation of energy and onslaught of ache and cough and the "I've never felt this awful before" feeling.

Gosh, here I am in the laundry room. S l o w l y taking things out of the dryer. Fold a towel, just the way I learned in childhood. Feel the texture of things, the luxury of things being fresh again. Feel that a coral-colored shirt would be nicer than nightclothes, wouldn't it. Yes, I'll take vitamins again. Maybe empty the dishwasher, put things away. Pick up the cushion on the living room floor, sent there by a nesting dog in our prized old chair, forbidden to him till now.

The sense of "desperate" fatigue is gone. Soldiers at war feel this numbing fatigue sevenfold, a hundredfold, but it does not end like mine. Mine ends with mere hours of time. Not with death or surgery or medications or anything much at all. Just time and giving in utterly.

Time and giving in – and rediscovering the wish to fold laundry again, the simplest of homebody tasks. Thank you, thank you. ❖

One More Thing

Sometimes
100 tasks are possible –
Beckoning, pleasing,
The intentions
Of a happy morning
Of coffee, silence, sunrise
Of action, optimism,
Quiet pride.
Then comes the 101st –
Just one more thing
At the brink
And it is too much
Even to contemplate.
Even if the slightest,
The least, the lightest
Of new responsibilities,
It is one too many.
It topples the day.

Should

Today *I Should*
Water the plants
Write the notes
Fold the laundered sheets.

No, today let there be
Dry dirt, silence, wrinkles
Weary spirit.
I Want To will come
Tomorrow.

P48 Fresh Grace

By now I have Lost in my life:
Horses – jumping rails, herding cattle
Tennis – my killer serves, dashing saves
Bike rides – 30 miles of hills and downs
Running – easy early morning miles
Dog as exuberant companion
Four miles to my two.
I have lost parents, siblings, friends
Some strengths once assumed
And my naiveté – happily ever after
Now lives time-amended in my heart.

Thus my path over many seasons
Toward new ways Found by 80:
Calm from reservoirs filled over time
Anger swift to come and soon to go
Like summer thunderstorms.
Despair stealthily dealt, pondered
Sent packing by wiser mind.
Hope ever present in the miracles
Of the ordinary day, like sunrise
And snow angels and rabbit tracks
And the first sprigs in spring.

Life grace everywhere discerned –
Grandmothering, honoring, giving thanks
The zen of single-tasking, of being still
The gift in walking well, up stairs
And safely down again, across a room
Around a block, or lazing miles at a time.
Of reading immersed in the afternoons
Of happenstance talks in the market
Of out-and-abouts with friends and wine
Of quiet evenings in our chairs
Of good sleep and a daydream for tomorrow.

Esmeralda

Esmeralda entered my life soon after my tire rim submerged itself in a puddle far from home, in a torrent of rain. Scene: Heading back to Long Island after a Gma (grandmother) visit in Westchester. Neighbors Larissa and her son Sebastian (age two) had preceded her by minutes. Tamara (Triple A), Joshua (AAA tow truck guy), and Harry (gas station man) followed the submersion discovery. This was a chilling (flat tire far from home in cold wet weather) morning.

Within hours, the morning filled up with lessons in life. Good ones, actually.

First, drive my daughter to the train station Monday at dawn. It was stormy-rainy out and the customary ten-minute walk to was no-go. "Would you mind, Mom?" I was soon to be headed home anyway after a grandmother visit on Veterans Day – granddaughters off for school, parents working. Of course it was Yes.

Off we went trainward, my daughter driving. The steering seemed heavy, she noted en route. But hugs good-bye at the station, over-the-shoulder "Thanks for being grandmother yesterday!" and off to Manhattan she went and back to her house on a hill in Westchester I went. Time to pack up and walk my granddaughter to school down the hill, then head for home a peaceful hour away. But a "However" was in the wings. Esmeralda was a surprise in the offing and would soon be there.

Satchel packed and granddaughter at school, I am now homeward bound with windshield wipers on frantic. My stalwart Subaru Forester steering does indeed seem heavy. The car pulls to the right. Odd. The low pressure light is on, left over from a slow-leak tire check the day before: the familiar old "rust on the rim" left-front-tire situation. "Well, all four tire pressures checked out fine just a day ago, the light will go off soon, but isn't it odd," said Denial to me. Three minutes later a hill-bottom puddle would yield the However.

But first: in my pre-puddle innocence, neighbors Larissa and little Sebastian had come over to see some new floor tile at my daughter's house; perhaps she would like to choose it for her house as well. Sebastian howled at the sight of me – tiny boy in his mother's arms, white-blond hair, anguished face, perhaps his mommy was going to leave him with me. But the tile was admired and Sebastian quieted. Larissa and I talked about tiles and blessings and my glimpse of her remarkable skills as an artist. Our talk was dear – one of those chance encounters that somehow leaves you pleased and soothed.

For some reason we touched upon anxiety, Larissa and I – the kind that I always feel setting out on highways via unknown roads, and she feels in her own life sometimes, as do we all. She showed me the sign language gesture for expressing anxiety, worry: head lowered, both forefingers turning slowly on each side of the eyes. The same gesture we all as kids once conveyed with just one hand circling, "She's crazy!"

But Larissa's was a gentle gesture. It conveyed the sense of personal chaos needing help, expressing a feeling of need and in doing so bringing calm. This was a quiet gift for which I said thank you, a gift I would like to keep in my life. Sebastian by now knew that his mommy was not leaving, and he waved good-bye to me, and repeated his mother's "Good bye, Terry" in his tiny Sebastian voice that melted my heart.

Within minutes it was my turn to leave my daughter's house too, en route home to Bob and dogs and my favorite chair. I turned off house lights, checked for forgotten belongings, and pulled the heavy door tight. Time to GPS my way out of the neighborhood's handsome warren of hills and winding roads.

How could I have been so dense? Two blocks and three minutes away, soon to hit the Saw Mill River Parkway, it came to me, dunce. Time to check the tires and make sure it's just the rain and the sodden leaves and I'm just dreaming about the heavy steering.

Which of course I was not. Not dreaming. But it took me a moment. The right front tire seemed submerged in the hill-bottom puddle. The Anxiety Devil began its work. "I'll back up and be sure it's just the puddle," said Denial again to me. This could not be.

And that was the end of happy days away delighting in the next generation. Disbelief, damn, what do I do?

Take a deep breath, call my daughter on the train, what's your local gas station; no satellite signal here, down from the hills.

Back up the hill to the house, hell with it I'll drive on the rim, dive into calls for assistance. All suggestions helped blessedly, one by one.

First the gas station and Esmeralda at Straub Auto – "We are close, we can come, please tell me address and best telephone for you." No, she didn't need my credit card number, when I offered. "Thank you but no, just the gesture is appreciated."

Then a call to AAA – that chunky red-white-blue plastic card I've never used but carry anyway just in case. Tamara at Triple A was kindly – "The tow truck can be there in about forty-five minutes. You'll be fine . . . " Her calmness was a gift.

By now of course I was in the crisis mode that I'm so good at after fifty years of marriage and motherhood's this or that – broken arms, falls, faintings, ambulances, surgeries, et al: keep it together now, come apart later. Good plan.

Tamara's promised tow truck driver Joshua arrived on cue – after some efficient texted "updates" (reschedulings and confirmations) – with the biggest and shiniest tow truck imaginable. Here was power in chrome, red, black, flashing lights, a mile long it seemed, all the bells and whistles. The thing I'd seen so often by the side of the road was now right here helping me. Helping. Me.

Joshua spoke to me from his truck, I at his side window rolled down. Swarthy handsome young man in yellow-orange slicker for safety and wet weather work, I the upset grandmother standing in the rain.

"You'll be fine. I'll just check your tire and we'll head to the gas station. I know the guy. Good man." Whereupon I poured forth my gratefulness and my upset, my elder status, my fellow elder at home, and teetered on the brink of tears. Someone was *helping me*. My whole gallery of people helping me this morning swept on in. Joshua's kindly reassuring words put my composure further at risk. But a deep breath worked and calm came. He could tow me, try air in the tire and see if it held, put on the spare and check it, anything, we'd figure it out.

The rest was just amazing. Joshua put two big blasts of air in the tire – two seconds' worth it seemed – and now there was a fat tire good enough for the trip to Esmeralda at Straub Auto. He and I discussed life for a minute. He loves his work and his truck (as who would not, with a truck like that), I love seeing my grandchildren, we both have blessings in our lives. A kind of quiet connection took place. Yes he would lead me to the gas station, and yes he could back out of this hill-edge winding one-lane dead-end road where my car was, when I asked how that would be. "It's fine. I have five eyes," he said.

Back out brilliantly he did and lead me he did, to his friend at Straub, and stopped to show me where to enter a labyrinth of cars parked every which way. No charge for AAA. We shook hands and said thanks for our time and the tip, and off he went. Good man, good help.

Now to Straub's Esmeralda, via Joshua's friend Harry. Harry had been expecting me, told me where to pull the Subaru, confirmed the tire's need, and sent me in to Esmeralda. Esmeralda of the calming voice. Brown haired and pretty, young, soft-spoken, good at handling big deliveries of tires and oil cans and car parts from a tiny office with customers waiting and invoices to sign.

Through all, I stayed in touch with daughter, gas station, and Triple A. Even Larissa and Sebastian offered help. My hope and confidence were ebbing back. The way was clear: Harry would find the tire's offending nail, plug it or patch it, and home I would go. Which is what happened.

"No charge," said Esmeralda with wave of hand. Harry likewise. Good heavens. I gave a tip of thanks and clicked on my friend GMaps for departure directions. Wi fi for GPS was needed in this Hudson River Valley location, so with Esmeralda's wi-fi I found my route and on my way I went. GPS quit me a few times along the hilly Hudson shore, but Saw Mill – Cross County – Hutch – Throgs Neck – Long Island Expressway saw me safely home.

Home safe. What a lovely term. Time to stretch out in my chair by the window. And reflect. The kindliness shown me, the efficiency of this whole network of help from strangers who care, a very good thing just now.

PS Yes there is a definite "TMI" aspect to the travail and kindness story here. Hello, it's just a flat tire. Yet it is a "heaven in a grain of sand" story as well: kindnesses to a stranger (me) are heartening in all directions. And, in googling the spelling of Esmeralda (is it *el* or *al*?) I learned that the character Esmeralda, in Hugo's 1831 *Hunchback of Notre Dame*, is a young girl with "a kind and generous heart." ❖

Why?

My role in life:
Live, learn,
Be a mother
And a minister.
Why?
It comes clear
Only now.

The Girl in the Blue Dress, Dancing

Just yesterday, as if newly born, something unfamiliar and beautiful came into my spirit. Actually there were two things yesterday – the old and the new. The old – seeing again the masks, urns, and dinosaur skeletons at Manhattan's Museum of Natural History. I've been a member there since childhood, far too often in absentia. The new is a glimpse into another life, as if a sheer curtain of sky and cloud hung down from the heavens, and I could look through a vertical tear, into beyond.

In my memory now and forever is a young Alaskan girl in a blue dress dancing almost motionlessly, moving her hands in an age old way suggesting polar bears, arrows, babies, the tiny motions conveying honor to the customs of her life. She wore leggings beneath her dress. She stood on a sealskin stretched smoothly in the Dance House for this traditional purpose. She was surrounded by women seated on the floor with legs out straight, men on benches behind them. The warmth of enclosure and families permitted thick parkas to be shed for the time.

The girl's face was stilled amidst her concentration. A bashful smile stole in now and then – she was dancing for the first time in front of all, and a documentarist's camera was permitted to be present.

The film, I felt on this day, was the documentarist's gift of knowledge to all present for this showing at the Museum. A glimpse, intimate and memorable forever, into the life of "The Elders in the Yup'ik village of Emmonak, Alaska," way north on the coast of the Bering Sea. The documentary was ten years in the making (planning, funding) and completed forty years ago in 1985. "The Drums of Winter" is its quiet name. Unassuming name, sacred message.

Step back a day. I almost missed it, the film. Family matters made the dawn-hour train to the city a challenge. But concerns of family and train time came to naught and there I was on the Number 2 train uptown just as intended. I secured a small $2.73 kiosk coffee at Seventy-second and Broadway, then sat on a bench to watch passersby until my fellow film-goer arrived. Meanwhile I loved the mini-gift of a father skipping by with his daughter. Two personifications of joy.

Then it was five blocks to the Museum, farmers' market goods arrayed en route for our savoring. Then inside for our tickets. They were held at "the Participants Desk beneath The Great Canoe." The canoe was indeed Great: it filled the entire room overhead – no way to miss it. Who once paddled it and where, and when? How many oarsmen did it take? The first of the Museum's infinite many marvels, that room-length canoe, once a single tree carved for new purpose generations ago.

We reached the theater via labyrinthine corridors led by docents with digital devices, passing by infinite ancient marvels on shelves and ceilings. No time for these on this day. Seated, we entered an hour of dimmed lights and life as we had never known it. We, sophisticates as we see ourselves, know nothing of this particular eloquence, this custom never dreamt of in our own narrowed lives: the tradition of drumming and dancing amongst the Alaskan Elders of the Yup'ik community.

The film itself was thrice honoring. It honored the Yup'ik dancers and drummers by respectfully capturing this private, nourishing time. The dancers and drummers in turn honored the documentarist, sensing her grace of spirit and permitting her to be present and to film. And we, the film-goers a lifetime later, felt honored by the documentarist's tender gift to us.

So many intimacies –

The Dance House itself with small door through which each participant bent low to enter from ice and blown snow outside . . . the fur-topped sealskin boots worn by all, each ornamental in personal design . . . the parkas themselves – fur-lined at hood and hem, white, blue, plain or all-over designed, all pullover so no buttons to let in icy air, no two alike.

And the Elders' faces – tanned and creased by wind and work, smiles reflecting the deepest joy, the knowledge of sacredness. The younger women seated around the circle of dancers, their own hands moving meaningfully as the day's participants too, or in memory of their own times as newest dancers. All in roomy patterned dresses and leggings, all upright in their floor places, each conveying via smile the joy of the moment or the warmth of the calming recollection.

As for the drumming itself, the instruments are flat – each a sealskin stretched taut to a round bone frame, like an expanded embroidery hoop. In preparation, each drummer touched the stretched skin with what seemed a moistening oil, tapped almost-ready sounds with ready fingers, and began. The pace was slow at first, a ritual quietly welcomed. In the center, seated cross-legged, young male dancers moved to rhythm with gathered feather and tooth and fox-fur tokens – a carving of the face of a bear with tiny ivory eyes on this one, perhaps an image of a seal on another.

Then the drummers' pace quickened, slowly at first then frenetically – the seated male dancers moving and turning and flinging arms in all directions – the wilder the movement the better the dance, we learned later from an Elder speaking of the way of the ritual.

The spirit of the Dance House drumming and dancing is, the Elder explained, a sustaining one. Through the hardships of climate – gales of winter wind and snow in darkness and bleakness – the families take nourishment from their ways of life.

At film's end we all just sat there, stunned by the beauty and intimacy of what we had just seen, and thirsty for details. Funding difficulties had delayed filming for years, we learned . . . the Yup'ik drumming tradition had been lost for years but today is quietly being reawakened within the Yup'ik community.

Certain unconnected memories stay with me from the film itself: The Yup'ik diet was predominantly meat for obvious reasons – no gardens or fruits or harvests are possible in forever-frozen land. So when berries come in via trading they are the dearest of luxuries. Boxes of Kellogg's Corn Flakes appeared on sleds from trading, with split firewood from distant trees.

. . . An archive of earlier French missionaries shows their late 1880s judgement of these "dirty people" practicing "Devil worship" and "lacking in the intellect we need for Catholicism." "They are so stupid they give everything away." Yup'ik tradition was to give all away as needed within and beyond their own community, thus no one starves. How zealous the missionaries' intention then, how blind today.

. . . In the film we saw nothing of Yup'ik lifestyle otherwise – dwellings, health concerns, children leaving for school in the wider world, all else. We did not learn of the impact of boarding schools and the ensuing deliberate suppression of the Yup'ik language, and that the dance had since nearly vanished. The documentarist's gift to us was concisely the experience of this community's custom of dance and drumming. We recognized it as holy gift.

. . . The film won awards in the Museum's Margaret Mead film festival forty years ago, and has been shown again since. It has been accepted by the

Library of Congress with its stringent standards, and its documentarist was named honorary archival film director for 2018's festival. In large part because of "The Drums of Winter" film, the drumming and dancing ceremony is being revived and "flourishes in a remarkable renaissance."

The telling thing for me, in my own scripted life, is that I knew nothing of the girl in the blue dress, dancing. She danced in my lifetime, as her drummers made their slender sealskin drums and the Yup'ik families exchanged gifts with neighboring communities and lived their lives of harsh climate and plain deep spiritual ways, and still I knew nothing.

The documentarist is in fact my friend of many years Sarah Elder – her name resonant with the traditions she filmed. We have discussed life intently, Sarah and I, and I had known of her film skills and of her long spells way north in Alaska. Yet still I had known nothing – until the glimpse through the sheer curtain of sky and cloud hung down from the heavens – of what lay beyond. ❖

Spathy & Philo

It sounds like a morning talk show in Greece: *Spathy and Philo, Live, from Athens!*

And in a way it is.

Each morning, I greet my loyal and hearty Spathiphyllum plant, lush dark green, and its sister-in-green my Variegated Philodendron. My eyes and heart give the greeting. And sometimes I even say Good Morning out loud – to the day, to life, to the everyman plants. Sprightly foliage, welcoming the early light. Leaves of that great dark shiny green that says "I feel great."

This is not to say that every morning begins this way. Sometimes I pay for the laziness of the days before, when even the smallest effort was beyond possible. These two loyal plants sag, hang down their heads as if in sadness, joined by drooping sister cyclamen, oxalis, and geraniums. That's a grim sight in my Sun Room and I have asked for it. They and I are thirsty and our needs have been unmet.

Always, always, however, I do rush to the rescue and water them faithfully again, glad at last to tend to the wreckage of my neglect. And always, always, they forgive me. How could they? But they do.

The Spathiphyllum came my way in forgotten fashion. It has been in the corner white wicker planter for eons and it has survived the droughts. When happy it shoots up tall little white flowers shaped like the upheld palm of my hand, with a centerpiece offshoot of tiny white nuggets.

Lo and behold one day recently, the blindness of familiarity lifted. On a whim I researched my tried and true Spathiphyllum to find the Latin source of its name. I did find the etymology (below) but I also found fifty treatises on the care of this unprepossessing greenery for which I had felt my own fondness all these years. It was like reading a book that I loved, and going to hear the author talk and finding I did not like her, so successful and innocence-lost was she. Just plain TMI.

Let that go, I vowed. *My* humble Spathiphyllum is like no other.

I did find a surprise about my faithful friend: It is also called The Peace Lily. Yes, the tall stemmed flowers do resemble Calla Lilies. I had never thought of that. Fresh news of an old pal.

Why Peace Lily? Apparently, it is said, "They were first spied by European explorers, probably growing wild on the banks of a stream, the white flowers reminiscent of the traditional white flag used to signal no combat or surrender." Doesn't that soothe the soul?

I took a treasure hunt to find how Spathiphyllum's formal name came about. Spathi, from the Latin *spatha*, for blade, is "a large sheathing bract that encloses a flower cluster." Yes sheathing, yes enclosing a flower. But what's a bract?

Bract is from the Latin *bractea* down from Greek, for thin plate of metal, and means modified leaf. That works: a flat leaf becomes the curvaceous lily. And Phyllum simply means foliage. So my ordinary Spathy is extraordinary in how it does what it does: survives drought (luckily for me, only the lightest of watering is recommended), stays a great green all winter, and when happy produces flowers that make me happy too.

Now to the special sister who survives my inattentions also: my pot of Variegated Philodendron, grown from cuttings and a cut above the usual plain green variety. There is something about this perky plant. Everybody has one – it is easy, pretty, resilient. Its cuttings sprout roots robustly and take to planting in ordinary pots of ordinary soil. Water is all they ask.

I have seen the plain green version in drycleaners, suffering near the window (mine doesn't like full sun either). And I have seen it also ignored and scraggly and pale and dusty on the sills of diners – perfect clime for losing their largest and innermost leaves and going leggy while the fresh young outermost leaves go right on recreating themselves as if nothing were wrong.

But my Philodendron is variegated – soft whitish streaks within strong green leaves, every last one actively the parent of a look-alike successor. That's amazing, really. How does nature arrange all that?

My Variegated Philodendron is forgiving and giving both – tiny scrolled-up leaves are always in line to open. Every day, baby foliage progressing. I've had its ancestors for forty years, provenance unknown. Philos means loving. Dendron is from the Greek for tree. Little loving tree.

Online tells me – horrors – that Philodendron is toxic to dogs; I never knew that but fortunately our dogs have never gone after them. Shoes and table legs, yes. Sliced chicken on the counter edge, yes. But Philodendron leaves right there in a red clay pot on the red tile floor, no.

I learned also that there are seemingly a million varieties of Philodendron – four hundred species! Take giant split-leaf. Take some with "golden yellow" striations (how awful, when you really love the dark green kind), or pointy, lacey, heart shaped, shrub sized, aborescent tree-like sorts, and on. Enough! Take me home to my humble ten-sprig pot of cuttings that sits on the floor and quietly makes gorgeous leaves, each the same as its cousins in another pot across the room.

And something delightful shows up in still a third pot of Philodendron: this one a miniature white Limoges porcelain cachepot, with one cutting in it that has branched to three. It sits on the kitchen counter with its three little sprout lengths outstretched. One day I noticed that each sprout length keeps itself an eighth of an inch off the counter, stems straight up toward window light, by creating what are in effect little feet all along the way. The very same "feet" that help Philodendrons climb up a wall, help it stay uprightly off the kitchen counter for a sprout's full length. I thought that was pretty cool, so sent a photograph of this phenomenon to my granddaughters. Tiny miracle shared.

So why do I do this horrible thing of neglecting my plants? Of seeing them drooping a bit, then worse the next day, then sometimes to the point of blossoms wilting before their time, of leaves putting their heads over the edge straight down? It is kind of like letting library books be late. I can do that without consequence – just pay a late fee to a place I love. It is not a 911 call and ambulance ride. Or an urgent vet visit for our dog. Or a promise to a friend. Each of these must be honored. Appointments, promises, deadlines, things I *must* do.

My rush to the rescue of Spathy and Philo and their Sun Room friends is, I recognize, a form of mutual replenishment and forgiveness. It pleases the plants of course. But it comforts me too after long days or wearying times. I can do this. Morning is coming. Things will be OK. ❖

Muddled 2020

Betwixt and between
Befuddled. Muddled mind.
Why now? The year is 2020.
Six weeks into this journey,
That terrifying surprise
Of corona handwashings
And isopropyl disinfections,
That confusion stage,
That mind-bending stage,
Seemed a thing of the past,
A waystation long ago left.

Why the return today?
"I don't want to play this anymore"
Has hit
Hard
Hell with it
Sick of it
Spray the cartons on the porch?
Wipe down the banisters?
Wash the bananas?
Soapy water for apples?
Who cares?

Soon I will gather my wits again
Dare again
Be of service again
Honor the brave,
The horrifically less fortunate.
Send modest money to hospital,
Times Neediest, local pantry.
Today I am bewitched, again
By the enormity of this moment
In time.
In my life time.

The Old Ways 2020

The sun has set on the old ways –
Strolls with friends, grandchildren grabbed
For hugs, go-to-hell gimlets at the local bar,
All our silly ordinary ways of being.
Today's fears and deaths will yield to time, yes
And subside within our Earth's eternal histories.

Yet it is this today, this afternoon, this dusk
That strikes night fears
That tells true colors
That quietly rearranges infinitely all.

Please, may the world's new ways reflect
Not the obscene behaviors of some
Not the day's deceits and disappointments
But the moment's kindnesses and courage.
May the sun rise on this new garden
Of decent, beautiful behaviors.

Corona Solo

Note to self:
I didn't mean to
But yes I'd love to
More wine
Extra chocolate chunk
That other item
In the catalog
It feels so good
To go to hell a little
To color outside
The self-drawn lines
Even slightly
Let's do it again
Tomorrow!

2020 Mother

Out in the back yard,
Euonymous is swathed
In lush green sprouting
Perfectly, uniformly.
Is this my last view
Of spring perfection?

Out front, Acer Rubrum
Maple branchlets
Put forth red shoots
Soon overwhelmed
By green successors, I know:
A yearly miracle.
Is today my last seeing such
Gloried transformation?

By executive order
I am housebound
So savor grandchildren's
Faraway laughter and smiles
Sent to me in digital magic.
Are corona days my last
For blown kisses
And ethereal hugs?

Today is the day of daffodils
Laughing and dancing
In the way of poetry.
Perhaps it is my last day of daffodils.
Please, corona, if you come –
If you seek my children,
My grandchildren, innocents
Let it be me instead.

I am every 2020 mother
Every settler mother
Every medieval mother
Every cave dweller mother
Quietly pleading thus.

A Walk 2020

Mid-May morning
My grandson is ill
Is it deadly?
Fear engulfs
Say nothing more
Do nothing more
Seek to feel
Nothing more
Read, hide, immerse.

After a time
Look beyond –
A glimmer
Walk anyway
Dog as company
Unaware, joyous
Meticulously
Investigative
Tree, grass, flower.

Look,
A child's rock, tiny
Curbside perch:
A rainbow in chalk
Walk on
A second rock:
"Hope"
A third:
A heart, and "Love."

My fear is present
Yet, impossibly,
Softer.

Whatever Happened
To Alice and Fredrica?

Remember that aching-anguishing feeling at the school dance, when He cuts in? Or does not? That old-fashioned practice of "cutting in" – so bold and honoring, so over today except for fathers and brides? A not-nice version of the opposite, I now understand from my friend Alice, is "cutting out."

Into life's dances with friends come mysteries big and small. Yes. Conundrums that baffle and bother. Mostly, these are moments briefly startling and soon resolved, the fretting all for naught. Or questions asked and answered or never asked at all and anyway lost in time. Alice, a childhood friend who lives far away and with whom I have kept in close touch over the years, told me of one mystery that has stayed mysterious.

It seems that Alice and her friend Fredrica were once as close as close can be – youngish mothers discussing life. They went for healthy striding walks, mentioned their own hopes and their children's dreams. Confidences were shared and privacy was always honored. Sometimes on wicked afternoons the two walked around their neighborhood blocks, white wine in old pewter cups, laughing hilariously at nothing, sure that nobody could ever tell why.

The two had met in the local church choir, a family in itself, Sundays divine and shared. Alice was a soprano and Fredrica an alto. Tenors and basses balanced their groups in music made with joy.

Once Alice and Fredrica took a trip north to relax in a farmhouse, gloriously away from life's concerns. They read or went their own ways by day, checked on children at home, and met up for dinner and fire and wine and talk at night. Early to sleep, up early, more walks, praise be.

Alice has a lovely autumnal shot of Vermont leaves, resplendent edge to edge, which she took one day with Fredrica's camera, just for the joy of it. Fredrica, the skilled photographer by profession and with the generous heart of friendship, made her a grand print of it – sharp blue sky setting off the glory of the leaves in red-yellow-gold and remnants of green. Alice framed it for its own beauty and for the beauty of the gift.

It was all telephone and mailbox note back then, twenty or so years ago. None of the ease – or psychological distance – of today's instant texts and flying-fingers emails. Today the ball is in the other court in seconds; a reply is a diss if not sent in the next minute.

Walks and talks and trips and books and laughter, Alice and Fredrica – a lovely easy friendship of many years, years ago. Then one day, and then the next week and the next, Alice's telephone calls began to go unanswered. Messages left. Notes left. Silence so odd. Was Fredrica all right? Depression? Family matters? Alcohol? What gives?

Soon three more fellow Fredrica cast-offs became known – a quartet of longtime friends cut cold by fiat, it seemed. They asked a mutual friend about Fredrica, concerned for her. "Oh, she's alright. She's just like that."

Each cast-off felt the rebuff. The rejections were confusing and hurtful. Questionings among the four: can you come up with anything? What event, what remark, what negative do we have in common?

Time stretched out in silence. Alice's response ran the gamut: hurt, anger, puzzlement, limbo. Fredrica made polite small-group conversation at a local garden party and Alice in seconds went elsewhere in the garden. Wound unhealed.

After a time, months of living life and still unenlightened, Alice put paid to it all. In a final postcard she wrote to Fredrica: "I do not understand the silences, but I wish you well in all things." Done. Let it rest.

In retrospect, Alice surmises, perhaps it was Fredrica's time for a new lease on life. Time to declutter. Simplify. Wheat and chaff time, with the quartet of old friends now chaff. Perhaps it's like going through your wardrobe, your *bureau drawers, as advised by the New York Times bestseller The Life-Changing Magic of Tidying Up.* "If something doesn't touch your heart, get rid of it now." "Quite freeing," this exercise, notes the book. We four were clutter now.

No matter the "why" of Fredrica cutting Alice out abruptly in silence, the act is of course not unfair, not earthshaking like the world's true heartaches and injustices. It is a small thing, a peppercorn in the great scheme, a mere iota, a betrayal of the commonest sort.

But Alice, who has lived joyously and held her grandchildren and made peace with the cutting-out incident of years ago, will never forget it. ❖

Ode to Coffee Grounds

Yes I do salute you
Every little rich brown
Powerful speck of you.
Today I beg your forgiveness.

In unraveled haste this morning
I left some higher level
Specks out of the pouring loop.
We had once achieved Zen,
You and I, in morning coffee.

With quiet care and deft hand
I had vowed to honor
Your wish to give your all
For the divine taste so essential
For daring my day.

Yet today, I poured silly fast
And left some of you
High and dry in the filter.
I here promise better
For tomorrow's morning.

Please, forgive my lack of grace.
I have the best intentions.

Ali & George

Two chance encounters, black and white in twinned ways.

Ali is a street vendor selling hats and scarves on a street corner in Manhattan – Forty-fourth and Sixth. George guides shoppers in the plumbing department of a Long Island Home Depot – everyone gets lost in that gargantuan place.

Ali is a hefty mustachioed black-brown man and George is medium height clean-shaven white. Their skin colors differ from each other. In turn, their lives could not differ more from mine.

Ali I encountered one cold day last week, when wind whipped the City's streets with extra strength in the corridors of the avenues. Fifteen degrees cut to icy-seven in the winds.

I had just left lunch and wine at the New York Yacht Club, that prestigious place with mahogany paneled Model Room and red-runnered marble stairs. It's where the America's Cup trophy shown silvery in its NYYC pride-of-place glass shelving, until we lost it years ago to Australia. That Fateful Loss of 1983, after one hundred thirty-two years of prideful winning.

Privilege – the well-earned maritime-social sort – is present at the Yacht Club. The nation's most notable yachtsmen belong there. I have been inside often over the years – guest status only, to understate – for my work in the maritime world. I am comfortable there by now yet always in awe. This time was for lunch with the wife of a late and brilliant NYYC member, remembering old times. Dear occasion, staff as always gracious to outsiders like me.

For the cold walk down from Forty-fourth and Sixth to Penn Station at Thirty-second and Seventh and the train home, I had zipped up and gloved for the elements. And there was Ali, jacketed and hatted himself, selling his multi-color array of scarves, hats, gloves, and related warming enticements.

I stopped to see the scarves – the familiar five-dollar Pashminas all cellophane encased and aligned in the latest pastel shades. Soft blue and deeper blues here, teal green here and lightest celadon green there, with neighbors of pink, yellow, and lavender. A palette of scarves for a windy City day.

Ali accepted my five dollars for the pale turquoise scarf that I had chosen. "Double?" he asked.

"I have a hat," I said, misunderstanding his Middle East accent to be suggesting a burquah sort of arrangement.

We straightened it out, when in gentle gesture he doubled the scarf and placed it above my shoulders, pulling the end through and snugging it all up for warmth. His own hat's fleecy earflaps and parka kept him okay for the long street-corner hours. We exchanged smiles and a nod. Transaction complete. There was a touch of love in our smiles.

I thanked Ali for his kindness and in parting asked his name, told him mine, and walked down Sixth Avenue warmed by scarf and encounter. I will never know if he has a wife and children. What hobbies he has. If he enjoys or resents the setting up and taking down of hats and scarves and gloves so artfully arranged, every day. What did he know of my Yacht Club lunches? My good fortune in life? That I had been brought up to wear white gloves on the subway and attend secret Junior League teas? Oh my. Save me from myself.

George of our local Long Island Home Depot entered my life the very next day. A go-do-your-errands day. My husband Bob and I were there to find a faucet handle. No luck. And Bob had gone off looking for a fascinating something else. But wait. What do I know of faucet handles?

George saw my road-rage face and offered friendly help: "Did you find the fixture you were looking for?" He was in a whole other place in his life vs mine – he not yet senior, seemingly beaming in good health, perhaps newly

retired from a career in science or carpentry. His orange Home Depot apron gave his name and beneath it advised us all to "Be kind." His good nature mismatched mine, which was stormy over a delay caused by life: Stormy? Impatient? Slow-striding spouse with Home Depot cart serving as his walker? What was I thinking?

George found the plumbing fixture we needed and we talked a bit while my Bob-with-cart went down still another aisle seeking fascinations: he loves hardware and tools and Home Depot is indeed an intriguing place. George himself looked as if he did know a thing or two about life. Perhaps open heart surgery or other near-miss event had opened his eyes to the more important things in life. I myself felt like an idiot. Here was the young-mother "fish-wife voice" I had once used with our children. Loud angry words then, silent foolish fury now. End-of-the-tether behavior then and now.

We talked of this and that, George and I. I asked about his apron's "Be kind" advice. He had once taught Eagle Scouts, he said, and a poignant response stayed with him. He had once asked one of his Eagle Scout graduates what he most prized from George's years of teaching: "Tolerance" was the treasured response. Caring teacher rewarded, in the grace of a child.

Before long Bob reappeared. By then I had "turned it around" – recognized my behavior as ridiculous and just plain mean. Idiot me. Get a grip, you old grouch.

To my Bob I offered an apology. To George I said, "I was meant to meet you here, today, this moment." He nodded yes.

To my little ten-inch wooden statue of St. Francis of Assisi, bird on shoulder, greeting me pacifically every morning over coffee and reminding me to look out yonder, I said "Thank you." ❖

My Bower

In country after country
Every morning more, more
Plain people, fancy people
Fathers mothers sisters brothers
Aunts uncles old young newborn
Stricken in the year's relentless
Death march, grim, earth-wide.

I mourn the sweet pigtailed girl
The grandmother alone
The tanned, striving field hand
The wearied nurse at risk
The handsome father of three
Innocent, brave, gone.
The hurt is keen in my heart.

Yet
I see bright prospects
On a Sunday morning in May.
Sunlight streams my street
I can walk in dreamy solitude
Go sit by the calming shore
See my grandchildren by laptop.

And I can escape in poems
Scratch my dog behind her ears
Immerse in murder mysteries
Struggle over crosswords
Clear a tide of ordinary clutter
Tend to laundry, kitchen,
Tasks long intended.

My cheering prospects:
How dare I have them
When the world, mostly,
Does not?

Anchorages

The other day I took my granddaughters to mini-camp at the local beach. Beautiful morning, smallest breeze, boats all at peace at their moorings, my snack-bar coffee in hand in the quiet of the day. Halcyon moment. I relaxed in an old white metal chair, iron and filigreed, with yellow porch shingles at my back and the whole harbor before my eyes.

The boats were quiet and all bows looked obediently south on their mooring lines. The tide was going out and the breeze was too soft in its touch for otherwise. More wind and they face straight into it; slack tide and stilled wind and they point every which way. These things I know from a lifetime of watching and savoring. Watching sometimes from the sand with our own children building sandcastles. Or sometimes at the end of a summer day aboard our old wooden ketch *Fayaway*. And always, the harbor offered surprises beyond these silent sparrings of tide vs breeze.

The boats are in a designated "special anchorage" – purple lines on the Coast Guard charts, depths noted, all vessels welcome. Launch service is upon request, modest mooring fees in the old tradition. But this anchorage is for me a treasure beyond the Coast Guard markings. It is the place where for years I have watched our babies play, sailed or skippered in races myself, identified squalls racing toward us in grey slanty sheets, doubled mooring lines against hurricanes, or, in utter otherwise, sat beneath a shading linden tree to read.

It is a safe place, this anchorage. It is familiar and comforting. It is history for me, for our family growing up and our children returning with children of their own. It is today a place to meet old friends or sit in blessed silence mulling over whatever presents itself. It is a place, a space, where I feel belonging.

Other places are my anchorages too – our house, our street, our town's historic shopfronts. And especially the local library – an efficient reference room table, a scrunchy leather chair by the fire, circulation staff who say hello when I enter. Church is the same, really – same pew from mere habit, same parishioners nearby for quiet greeting. Same silent glances of hello.

The ultimate anchorage, of course, is home. My husband of forever, my favorite chair in my favorite light-filled room, my own pillow and reading light just so. And, our two shiny black dogs whose eyes and tails convey their love so unmistakeably. Endless lovely lucky list.

For those who have no anchorages like mine today, however, my heart aches for their loss at sea. Their needs of which I am only distantly aware. My brain lacks a single detail of their lives. My thoughts go around the world in sorrow, for the deepest pain felt by displaced or never-placed persons elsewhere in this moment. I wish that somehow some kind of small miracle of comfort would happen. An angel nudge. A kindly glance from a stranger. A child adopted. A parent and child reunited. This is mere prayer. Idle thought, of no help to anyone, just the deepest wish.

In a three-sixty of thought, a local switch from wishing and remembering, my eye now goes back in time. From my white filigreed chair on the porch I see this slender geographic swath of shore of which I am only the latest occupant. Who before me has sat safely on that porch and mulled over life's concerns? Or watched squalls come south or whitecaps whip up and the boats respond?

And who before that has watched harbor weather come sweeping in – no beach house yet, perhaps centuries ago, perhaps a nook in the trees once lining the shore. Ours is a sheltered harbor, forested hills east and west, south an inner harbor shallowed and shoaled for harbor work, north exposed but free of rocks in a smooth glacier-carved entrance. And fresh water abundant and excellent, welling up in chilly artesian purity. Today this is our town Cold Spring Harbor.

Perhaps another woman sat in my place of today long, long ago, her face tanned and creased by time, thinking about children, sickness, sadness, the future, her hopes. Perhaps she was revered as an older woman, a custom rush-stricken from today's behaviors.

This harbor – this safe familiar place echoed elsewhere for others in other forms and times – is my belonging place. It is my anchorage, the literal and the mystical interwoven. ❖

Aging in Place 2020

Aging day by day
Aging limb by limb
Aging fear by fear
Never again handshakes?
Never again hugs?
My spirit shrinks
Where is Morning?

Toy Basket 2020

It has been so long
Since indoor visits from our
Grandboys and grandgirls
That they have outgrown
The toys in the toy basket.

Tell Me True, Damn It!

If ever I am led to pen a letter of Elder Advice for my full-grown children – parents themselves now and wiser than I ever was – it will touch upon memory and two related turns of phrase. And the letter will carry thanks and a plea.

The first turn of phrase is an instruction. It touched my own mother-child interactions every day from toddler to senior year, all occasions, all hours. I found the phrase in the one book that I ever read about child care (other than Spock when croup and projectile vomiting scared me into it): *The Magic Years*. The instruction: "Try to say yes."

It worked marvels. "Yes, good to go to the playground. It's raining now and this afternoon or tomorrow we can choose the best time." Or, "Yes, let's go get you some Goldfish – you get the Legos into the box and we'll go on down right after nap, OK?" We each got what we wanted, eager child and weary mother. Firm soft parental decision, no negative slap-down words.

The thanks are for this *Magic Years* instruction guiding me well as a mother, and for how I see it emulated in my children now as parents in today's swirling world. The words, the divine instruction, went smoothly into my brain the moment I read them decades ago. I see this non-adver-sarial way of resolving things guide the lives of our grandchildren and I am grateful. To my children I say: "I love to see how you are as parents." Our son and daughter are in the middle of life, working hard at their income-producing jobs. Going to soccer games and coaching baseball and encouraging Girl Scouts and neighborhood Secret Santas. Arranging good safe child care for the after-school work week. And, navigating the ocean of offspring requests in a firm, clear, and affectionate manner. My children are today where I was then, in the "Try to say yes" stage of life.

Then there is the other turn of phrase, the one with a plea in it, also a matter of memory. My own. My memory has traveled on to a later stage of life. It has weathered eighty years of 24/7 action and it sometimes falters. My friends have the falters too: Why did I come into this room? Where is my cellphone? Did I turn off the stove? Bob shares this in his way: Have you seen my keys? Where did you say you were going?

Well, all that is honestly fine. Sometimes hilarious. We are in it together. We can tell foolish stories over wine.

But here is the serious part. A plea to my children, regarding my story-telling or news flashes these days: *If I have told you the story before, tell me! If I have told you the latest neighborhood news before, tell me!* Stop me gently mid-sentence. Tell me true. Try "Yes, you mentioned that, Mom."

I recall a man at a bar in Pensacola, Florida. I was there to meet a Navy Captain helping me write about World War II aircraft carriers. Soon I would be interviewing senior Navy pilots about their roles in launching off to Midway. What an assignment.

At the bar, as I waited, the spry old soldier told me of his time on that freezing Ardennes trek in the Battle of the Bulge in 1944-45. I responded with a deeply felt, "Really? You survived the Battle of the Bulge?" He told me some details and clearly he welcomed this eager audience of one: me. I go back to that moment. How many other times must he have told his story – to new people, to the same people who may just sit there in boredom and finally say – "You told us that already, Dad."

And I remember my brilliant uncle telling and retelling me things. Doesn't he remember telling me that story last time? I remember. Why can't he?

Well now I know firsthand. No, he did not remember. And no, he likely, like all of us in the Elder-Brain set, could not. It is one of those skills – one of the infinite marvels of memory – that diminishes over time, or simply vanishes without trace. Was I *ever* able to remember who I had told what to?

That is where I am now. One small step into "slightly diminished." I have traveled from Child to Mother to Grandmother proudly silvered. In some ways I have traveled round to Child again, when our children help me resolve life's current conundrums.

And to this I say, to my dear Jenifer and Robert in their own middle stages of life, Tell me! Damn it, *Tell me if I tell you twice!* None of that daughter-to-son aside of "Mom told me about that time Marvin dog chased rabbits and wouldn't come in and they kept calling. . . . She told me twice. Did she tell you?"

None of that, please. No drumming your fingers hoping I will wind down. *Promise me.*

Just use gentle words early in the story: "Yes, Mom – you mentioned that." Nothing abrupt, nothing putting me down as an old codger who can't keep things straight. Just us, parent and child in the natural order of things. Recognizing that we are in this together bound by love.

It is all reminiscent of the gentle guidance from *The Magic Years,* wise-kindly words acknowledging who knows best and who is the parent just now. ❖

Trumpet Vine Time

It is the time of trumpet vines! The lovely soft white-and-yellow flower, the frolicky kind. Those blue hydrangeas and eager yellow-orange stands of day lilies share this month too. And, artfully arranged yellow marigolds, pink New Guinea impatiens, and the tall purple upthrusts of hostas.

It is late June now. The season of the Summer Solstice, the beginning of the loss of daily light a minute or so at a time.

Trumpet vines scent the air. They climb up and wind around the best-kept bushes. They send out tendrils that wave in wind and fasten on to whatever

shrub shoots they come upon – they even seem to travel from one bush to the next – do they go underground? Send seeds over? It's a mystery, one of a million-million of nature's own.

The vine I mention here lives just down the street, hitting my brain with its light bright-whiteness whenever I walk by in the mornings. If my daydreams are elsewhere when I near it, it tells me it is there. Admire me, it says. I am beautiful in white and yellow, don't you think? And breathe in, see what I can send to you through the air. Perfume. Slow your walk, savor me! And to the trumpet vine's entreaties I say Thank you, yes, I do see, you are indeed beautiful.

Trumpet vines are part of my fondest memories of youth. My father Henry planted some just outside a window near which we ate breakfast, lunch, and dinner in the summers away. He peered out often to check and sometimes yes hummingbirds were there. He was soft-spoken in his appreciations when this happened. I came to share his quiet joy.

Somehow these persistent vine-blossoms fell out of my caring for the next nearly seventy years. It is only this year, in grandmotherhood and pandemic era with our frightening world situation, that they reentered my life. Reentered on my customary morning walk – the same one I have taken for years without noticing a single trumpet vine. Happenstance? Gift from the gods on a thirsty day?

Yesterday, home from a perfumed reminiscent walk, I looked up Trumpet Vine – what is its history? Who else loves it?

Well, horrors. Google gave me only blazing red and strident yellow showings. "The trumpet vine is a root-hardy perennial into zone 8 . . . cultivated as an ornamental." Well, if this had been a book I would have snapped the covers shut with a whap. I clicked Home on my cellphone to banish the sight. I cannot unsee this violation of my sweet vision of my father and my youth, so I will just forgive it.

No matter. I found a good definition in the OED, a settling soothing honest one. "The trumpet vine is a climbing vine, a creeper." That's much better. I'll stay with the softer flower, the white-yellow old-friend one. It is as if twins took differing paths in life. One to the "well-bred" fancy nursery life as a bright red "climbing shrub" for gardens with edged green lawns and sprinklers. The other the "stay at home and work at the gas station" kind. That's my kind.

What to do about all this? Nothing at all. Savor the mornings. Look forward to the gift of scent and sight that will greet me tomorrow. ❖

Privilege

Privilege white
Privilege healthy
Privilege retired.

First coffee alone, quiet
In a big old house
Children grown, gone
Strong, happy.

First coffee, pondering
Sun lights the windows
And front yard hedges
Trees surround me.

I walk in my neighborhood
Solo, merely listening
Then home, second coffee
In morning leisure.

Ample generous scoopfuls
Teal coffee-kettle all mine,
A whimsical purchase
Just for its cheering color.

Pandemic
Sheds light
Black Lives Matter
Sheds light.

My privilege protects me
My privilege blinds me
In light, today
May my privilege
Help me see.

Low Morning 2020

It is a low morning
Sunless, the day itself dispiriting
So I go out for a walk
In search of small upliftings.

A fern! – New to me
In a neighbor's garden
How perfect its geometry
Fronds wide and lacey
In graceful easy arc.

The wild corner lot –
Weeds perfected by neglect
One Rousseauesque, elegant
Alignments spaced by God
Saplings and goatweed are near.

A hydrangea blossom –
As bold a blue as the ink
Of fountain pens
Outshowing its cousins
In pink and palid blue.

Hostas – clusters shaded
For just the right summoning
A long lush row at streetside –
Purple flowrets, bell on bell
Held on slender stems.

I am lost in thought now
In deep breaths and sighs.

Strawberries

Luscious red, perfect-for-summer berries in a bowl, sweetly moist and pleasing to the eye, and entirely misleading moonwise. . . .

The other night, outdoors for a front yard task, I saw the bright round radiant moon up behind the maple branches. I stepped left a bit to move tree leaves aside. Glorious orb, lighting up its sky. The next night would unbeknownst to me be the Strawberry Moon – the term famed to most but not thus far to me. But what a plain perfect glow, that sky on that clear predecessor night.

The next night, now in the know thanks to the evening-news meteorologist, I glanced up again but clouds hid the moon. It got me to mulling. Strawberry Moon – not the moon color at all, says the Old Farmer's Almanac! But the phase for the New England Algonquian's ripening crop, marked by June's full moon. Oh, the sun and moon and stars, guides to our forebears ancient and ever since: Harvest time? Sowing time? Winter shelter time? Monsoon or drought in the offing, as generations had recognized in the pattern of the years?

And before that, paintings in caves in France or libations poured at Greek ceremonial times, in joy or sadness or plea? Sun-moon-stars signal for behaviors down through time. Some things are eternal.

We have our own ways today in discerning the patterns of our years, different but the same. At Smith College, where I briefly studied philosophy and religion and English, each Fall brings a gift: Mountain Day. September's curriculum pressures do accrue and October brings splendid colors, so Smith honors a day – the date always a surprise – when blue skies and red-orange leaves conspire as a refreshing palliative time. The college president rings the campus bells to cancel all classes, and no papers are due for the day. We are each urged instead to go out and play – climb Mount Tom, go for a walk, take time for thinking. This a tradition for Smith's hundred and fifty years thus far. What wise soul first came up with it? Pressures then, pressures now.

Mountain Day is essentially a tesseract – a wrinkle in time, as Madeline L'Engle's book calls it – where you go off somewhere and come back and no time has elapsed. The actual physics explanation does exist but lacks magic for me so I pay it no heed.

So my newfound Strawberry Moon knowledge led to an interpretation all my own. Moon-sun-stars guide us infinitely – sleep in dark, wake in light, longer nights and shorter days or the reverse. I like to notice the changes surrounding our solstices. The flowers and all else notice too, in their ways.

Stonehenge reflects this celestial guidance so lost in our modern tech devices – sow, harvest, sleep, wake, pray. For years I've noticed the early light on our own street – morning sun streaming straight down Midland Street left to right past our house. Before many days pass I begin to see a slightly slanty light instead, and intrusion by the shadows of trees. It is an annual phenomenon, this golden streak for a week or two, a Neolithic-esque gift that comes when the time is right. It is brief yet it keeps its annual promise. Our Midlandhenge.

The Strawberry Moon occasioned my own tesseract – the proclaiming of a mid-June day in which all "should-do" tasks do not exist. Banish the towering Shoulds: I *should* straighten the linen closet, *should* clear up the office mess, *should* assault the tide of clutter on three floors of our very old house. And while at it I will banish the daily routine too – beds made, kitchen coffee ready, vitamins in their usual tiny anticipatory dishes, make a checklist for the day.

Aha! Clear the daily deck! Skip all this dreadful perfection!

Instead I stroll, disavowing the siren call of time and electronic items. Instead, I notice the little things. Break all possible rules. Feel free to do all the "do nots" – sit overlong (bad for circulation) . . . neglect to buy breakfast bananas (a solemn promise broken) . . . cross my legs in church (unprayerful) . . . eat a column of Oreos (definite shalt not).

And tomorrow morning, get up when I feel like it and wear what I like, shoes optional. Coffee first of course. Consider things. Sit outside in the bower – my Adirondack chair hidden beneath a yew tree, with a tree-trunk table and lily of the valley still sprightly in the shade. Write things in my journal – hate this, love that. Declarations in secret silent words.

After a while, as motivated, go indoors and straighten the old tugboat lithograph near the kitchen. Move the front door's big brass umbrella stand back where it belongs, just a few inches to the left. Honor the tambour desk's aged green velvet liner by tossing or stashing extraneous papers that hide it. Gather the remnant commemorative stamp batches – and use them with extra postage for the letters to grandchildren. Why not mail a whole package covered tip to toe in stamps? Outrageous. Splendid.

Do bother with the little things – antidotes to life's current complexities. Tend to the philodendron cuttings (their new roots have long earned the privilege of soil), the scuff mark on the radiator, the chip in the paintwork, the shredding edge of a carpet – scissors and two seconds and it's done. Best intentions, long left by the wayside.

In my mind's eye, lazing for a moment in my chair, move from room to room as armchair achiever: note the things I can actually do one by one on this day. So easy just now. So undoable yesterday in the impossible triage of weariness, spirit, enormity.

Just as my sister Elizabeth and I used to make lists and cross things off when achieved, *and* add unintended tasks retroactively and cross them off too – I relax at day's end and marvel at my Mountain Day, my tesseract time of small completions. I am rich in what I have done. Perhaps I will commemorate this day in new behaviors – read the classics at last, find a new kitchen cutting board, do some things differently, freshly at last.

So might the cave dweller artists have felt, the Stonehenge builders, the creators of sun dials, the sowers and reapers of crops, the bears and moles and voles and foxes wintering over, the whole membership in the cycle of life, and, on exactly this June day, the observers of the Strawberry Moon. ❖

How Is It ...

How is it …
… That one morning a tiny rose leaf, fallen and brown,
can cup a crystalline droplet the size of a moonstone?

… That ranks of yellow daylilies lean out in aligned perfection,
as if remembering yesterday's sun times and eager for today's?

… That two lawns - the browning have-not lawn and the
proud green edged-and-sprinklered lawn - can sparkle alike?

How? Well, it is the pre-dawn thunderstorm rain – the sudden
straight-down kind, full and heavy like a translucent theater curtain –
rushing from its clouds, sighing.

Ladies of Leisure of Yore

My mother had a happy life.
With her I knew of –
Victory Gardens & the privations of WWII
Secret teas for the Junior League
"Ladies of Leisure"
The McCarthy hearings &
the day Kennedy was shot.

In death she missed –
Her grandchildren &
the Double Helix discovery
The Vietnam War & Apple computers
My wedding, & all beyond.

In death my sister missed –
Robocalls & smartphones & texting
The 9/11 Towers day &
Sully's Miracle on the Hudson
Her children's weddings, & all beyond.

In death my brother missed –
Pandemic 2020 &
the brutalities of governance
Wilder wildfires & tornados &
self-driving semis
Holding his grandson a second time,
& all beyond.

In life I have seen –
Climate-strengthened hurricanes
& floods
Cyberwars & missions to Mars & Moon
My children flourish &
give us grandchildren.

In life I have not yet seen –
My five grandchildren's graduations
A blessed return to peace &
decency country-wide
The eventualities of climate change.

And I have hope for them all
In my future, & all beyond.

Honor the Upstarts
Of the Season!

In October, do you ever stop to notice the upstarts of the season? You see the rightful autumnal ruins of hostas, yes, but next to them the little white Queen Anne's Lace lookalikes stand fresh as daisies. They have proper names, these honorable weeds, but I do not know them. I simply salute them this morning.

As if setting the stage for surprise, down the block a trickle of water dribbles along below a sprinkler system truck; tis still the season for Scott-green lawns. Right behind the truck, handily in tow, is a little trench digger named Ditch Witch. Poetry in work.

Soon I see the milkweed that someone staked up to encourage its life and entice the mothering butterflies. It is looking peaked in seasonal struggle. Yet beside it I see a fresh new milkweed plant bigger than all the others and looking as if it just came into being. What happened here – a purchased plant? God? The new milkweed is greenly luxuriant in the Fall beside its Dregs-of-Summer sisters.

Down the way the invader vines appear proudly. The rest of a fancy shrub is showing its age – leaves thin, branches apparent. But the invader vines are shooting up as if they own the place. Sometimes they're the ones that the bugs go for first, the tasty vines, but this time they are the ones that jut out as egocentric statements, while the rest of the bush turns dim. Show over. The invader vines win the scene.

Now is also when the majestic spruces droop, but the variegated vines show yellow brightly as they thread through blue-green branches. And the tiny clover armies march right over curb stones and garden edges again fresh as can be. Did someone say summer is done? And I see poison ivy, fulsome but surely embarrassed. Its leaves have gone a weak yellow before its weedy surroundings even hint of the coming of fall and the red-gold glory of maples. And inter-brick terrace greenery – impressively intricate upstarts, weed-whacked the week before but fresh and forward again. How do they do that?

All around, if I look, I can see nature sneaking against the grain of its own plan. The time when everything is supposed to be shutting down. Over there, I see two other exceptions as Man has intended: season-defiant marigolds and banks of well-bred bold pink New Guinea impatiens. Even the last roses are still honoring summertime.

And I see also an eager gang of tiny spring-green Japanese lace maple leaves, sprung from the trunk itself near the ground, surely saying to themselves *I will grow up and be big too, and gorgeous red.* ❖

Oh, the Irony of Vision —
Eternal 2020

Mid 2020 – Covid 19 has hit the world, growing monstrously, killing incredibly, breaking spirits and hearts. Something awful is happening. Where are we going?

I am housebound in fear. Daring for me is a jaunt downtown for wine, masks for merchant and customer, please place in my trunk, thank you, bye. Our smiles are masked but seen in our eyes. This tiny spirit connection assuages my person-thirst, for a moment.

How long the fear? Half a year thus far, throughout our chilling March-April and all through hottest ever July and August. Another half year or full year or more or forever to come? Our breaths will coat our masks from the inside, come January. Six months, 180 days, eternal days still to follow. Isolation, deaths, malign behaviors, anxiety for country and the whole world. Will anything ever be safe for me? A dark rainbow shades all.

A youthful decision in favor of life does comfort me some, as it did one day sixty years ago. I walked down Fifth Avenue in New York, age twenty-two and despairing, to a free concert in the Frick Museum's frond-lush indoor garden. Along the Avenue way, perhaps from some source unbeknownst to me until now, came the light of recognition, the simplest of understandings: my happiness was my own responsibility. No one else's – not a friend's, not a lover's, not a stranger's, just mine. The purest gift of understanding, momentous and everlasting for me. OK that I would never find someone to love, someone to be loved by. OK that loneliness would be my path. There are riches in loneliness and I would find them.

And once loneliness was accepted as my prospect, it never did become my path. Awaiting me generously were books, music, friends, flowers, family joys yet undiscovered. Yes I was rich beyond measure.

A lifetime later as wife, mother, grandmother taking glory-walks in my neighborhood, I see friends albeit masked and I love sunlight in my windows and in my life. And I remember the Fifth Avenue day that changed everything.

So here we all are in Eternal 2020. Covid isolation, bizarre world governments, threatened planet, indecencies in the ascendency CNN reports. All touching every life on Earth. My grandchildren, who have just begun their lives, are among the targets of this hideously tangled situation. Despair waits in the wings. Yet, I know what to do.

Make peace first. Serenity Prayer peace: I cannot control these things. I will thus find "happiness" – peace – in fresh ways within this threatening moment of lifetime.

On my walks, I will check the Rose of Sharon sprigs, ready for August blossom.

In the mornings, I will ask my quiet Bob to tell me boyhood stories to write down, at last, for our children. Some hi-jinks stories seem more tellable now. Confessional time?

From my favorite chair, I will keep some hitherto unmet promises to self: add soil to the starving Cyclamen, write to my old friend Lucy, give some belongings away.

I will also do some routine things differently, just for the freshness of doing so. Walk earlier for the sole sound of birds. Yesterday's *Times* unread? Toss it; way tired and the hell with it. Buy Tate's caramel cookies and scarf a few. Sleep in my clothes. Write more love letters. All this and whatever playful, freeing else comes to my survivalist self, to outlast Covid and the evils of the 2020 day. ❖

Oh, Little Did I Know —
The Way Out 2021

September 2021 – On this Saturday morning I say a prayer to self, a questing thought about all this. What is the way out of relentless recurring fear? Out of feeling hopeless? I need to find it.

I go out walking at strolling speed, noticing the small familiar things. Then I overhear a father say to his young son, out walking too: "Look for something you've never seen before, and tell me." Father and son are in company of a little daughter-sister in a stroller, and a rescue dog named Mona, a dear old golden walking a little stiffly and not stopping to sniff things, just content in her foursome out for a walk near home. This small scene glimmers a way out of the gloom of the day.

Around the corner, my friends the luxuriant side-lot weeds have been sheared back sharply from summer over-stepping. I see fresh green sprouts emerging defiantly: "You can't stop us!" I say a silent hooray for them.

Across the way I see yellow marigolds at work protecting tomato plants against the rabbits. Every day is a natural contest.

I see no trace of an enormous pine tree felled in nor'easter wind just a week ago – mighty in girth and stretched way out along its lengthy lawn. Sleeping giant, a marvel gone. In its place is spacious smoothened ground within a low rock wall, readied for new plantings. Hope lives here.

I see a little girl in a blue flowered dress. It is the first day of September Kindergarten and she will meet her teacher but come right home. Just to begin this new life of going to school. Sweet-sized person, unaware of the lingering perils of the day. Her mother is aware. We are all aware.

I see a street-side basketball hoop with a new sleek grey fitting – a spoon-shaped contraption just under the netting, to guide the ball back out to the shooter's hands. Ingenious! What will people come up with of next? I am cheered by this cool new idea.

Today also I learn of two more years of elusive Covid variations. Today I ask – will I live out my grandmother days in resurgent constraints? Will I slide back into a desolation where nothing seems possible, not one thing? Pandemic2020 was heavy-going for me and tragic for others. Yes I will soon see my children and grandchildren again – we have already planned it for the back yard, mask-free! No more touch-free hugs! How I miss a child in my lap with a book. This "Soon" slid away and away again from that September day, the Kindergarten day. But it will come someday. Someday.

Yes, the way out of wondering and fearing – *The Way*, I now see – is to *act*. Over coffee, find some kindnesses to do and some gifts to give. Every day rain-shine-hot-cold go outdoors into thriving life and light. Go sit by the water, in quiet. Walk in the mornings and notice my neighbor guiding his son. Glimpse the sweet girl in the blue dress. Honor the valiant weeds and the new garden intended, succeeding a giant pine tree lost to time and storm. ❖

Openness 2121

It falls like gentle rain,
This openness, this reopening
To the old ways lost.
A return to the ways
Of unmasked smiles
Of daring to enter a store again
Of hugs, unmuffled words
Of hope showing
Of shopping for apples and breads.
It is elation, this returning,
Yearned-for openness.
The sun is rising and setting
newly. It is spring time,
All over green again.

As Silvered Elder...
What Should I Do Now?

Oh, I have seen the wounding of our beautiful democracy by elected liars, cheaters, and thieves. I have learned of oceans, countries, forests, and sacred natural places in ruins. With friends, I have felt grief and fear brought by losses of infinite kinds.

In photographs, I have seen a parent carrying a baby impaled by shrapnel. A refugee's child lying dead on a sandy shore. Bellies huge on starving children with innocent eyes, or ribs showing starkly on dogs and old horses that deserve better. I have seen the devastation of fires, floods, winds, and bullets – they are worsening now on our planet, and we can see them up close, instantly and intimately.

And I have seen "man's inhumanity to man" in play today in full color or ugly innuendo in newspapers, magazines, television, computers, and cellphones. I have not seen the numberless other awful scenes that doctors, soldiers, policemen, firemen, and others have seen and been shocked and shaped by.

But I have also heard a child's happy laughter from across the street.

I have seen a lone pink dogwood blossom in late September, looking angelic.

I have seen kind strangers help old ones step up a curb.

And I have seen a child be born, and minutes-old jet black puppies blindly climbing over each other to nurse, or a live giraffe birth made legendary by a 24/7 video-cam out west, just like the red-tailed hawks on a Manhattan windowsill.

What an incomprehensible array of sadness and sorrow and inexpressible loveliness. What should I do? What can I do? What is the point anyway?

"Just do today," someone once said to me on a rock-bottom day." Just do this one day, and then the next." Simple counsel, comforting. Take a deep breath.

There is naught for it, if I dwell upon the nadir strifes that are upon us now. If I succumb to sorrow and say Be done with it, End hope and chance, End effort, End trying. Just go adrift.

Or else, I can turn it around. I can take a chance, give a chance. Be invincible by decision. Count blessings. Trite terms, those, but the "succumb to sorrow" path is pointless, goes nowhere starting at dawn and going on forever.

So, I will just do today. Do some things differently. Notice. Listen. Go for a morning walk and weigh some possibilities for the day. Remember some decent things from yesterday. Vow "tomorrow I will..." Consider hope. Do a favor. Call a friend.

In fact, I am already invincible by decision (except sometimes when crawling under the covers seems the best option; that's okay occasionally too). I have made my peace with "the what is" in some places, with more peacemaking in the wings, at the ready. My blessings are boundless and they sustain me (our children, grandchildren, friends, house and home, health, books, crossword puzzles . . .) unless I forget to count them. Hope is there for the seizing –

I will write stories and it's OK if nobody reads them or cares.

I will write love letters and let everyone say I am mushy and ridiculous.

I will be of service in small ways and no one needs to notice.

I will go out and play as always and take a risk or two, and say hooray about it.

I will go for walks and dream things up, entertain possibilities. . . .

And I will read books long recommended by friends. Wear my size twelve pants and toss the tens. Eat lots of salad but go to hell sometimes too. Adore my children and grandchildren. Savor the life I've had with a good and kindly man, and tend to things medical as they arise at this fourth-quarter stage and so what for tomorrow. I will say good morning to the day. Water my plants and apologize to them when they droop in thirst. Marvel at the intricate pink-purple-white blossoms that cluster on my violets in their inadvertently perfect morning light.

And I will still, with the whole world, hear of horrific things local and global. And I will do my true best in light of it all, help as possible while keeping well, laugh in gladness sometimes, and take joy wherever I come upon it. ❖

Earth

Our sky is not infinite
In its resilience
Our seas are not infinite
In resilience
People are not infinite
In resilience
This we know now
Too late?
Earth needs
Stunning changes
At last
I need hope
For our children.

Go-to-Hell Friday

On this day,
Do no tasks
Solve no problems
Make no appointments
Clean no counters
Do no laundry
Return no calls
Muster no cheer
Find a book
Invite boredom!

Love II

Sixty years ago
And then some
I, lost and floundering,
Met a lawyer, a Yale man,
Tall and smart,
A federal prosecutor to be.
I met his father, handsome,
White-haired, kindly.
Bodes well for me –
Son will follow Father.
Son, strong and soft-spoken,
Will take care of me,
Love me true,
As I so needed, I felt,
In my infancy of insight.
Our wedding was tender,
A dream, friends attending
In my childhood church.

Today, I know more
Of love, the deeper thing.
Today, I am the stronger
In this our near-60th year,
Caregiver for the one
Who took care of me.
Difficulties, and then some,
Discovered and met.
Children grown and well,
Grandchildren growing well,
Pandemic life changing all,
Illnesses and imperfections
Surfacing for us both,
Friends sifted and stayed,
Favors asked and offered.
Every day I see new things,
Think new thoughts,
Discover intricacies of joy.
Today, in our reversals,
I know what love is now.

Azaleas in November

I went walking to find signs of spring, on a warm day
this past week. I saw snow drop sprouts, new yellow forsythia,
dandelion buds, onion grass, iris shoots, pachysandra blossoms,
perfect red roses, and a general greening and swelling of things.
A neighbor told me of pink hydrangeas blooming,
and a purple azalea. This week is Thanksgiving.
Nature is certainly tricky.

Seven Self-Servings
Of the Good Stuff

Tacky-dreadful days are old news for any of us. Days when all is amok from raccoons in the trash, to dissing (imaginary?) by a friend, to the hell-on-wheels times in Washington and the world these days. On one such subterranean day I took action. Find some good somewhere. Anywhere. Create your own aura. Seek out Seven Self-Servings of the Good Stuff, as it turned out.

Of course "self-serving" and "selfish" stand at a fork in the road of behaviors. The one suggests behavior at the expense of others. The other – the one I choose and cherish here – is the one too often neglected, the "care of self" behavior that I am at last discovering.

First on the subterranean day's agenda came a doctor's appointment ten easy minutes from home. One of a million such appointments in these grandmother years of mine.

In I went when called, after a brief wait during which odd sounds came from a wheel-chaired elder hunched over with her back to me, and a buxom beautiful Black aide murmuring calming nothings to her charge. What a life for them both, I was feeling.

Called in for my consult, and with counsel from the doctor accepted, I headed for the Exit door. I decided en route to say thank you to the receptionist in rapt consultation with her computer. Why not? Life is short . . .

"Thank you for always being pleasant with me," I said. "You all are so thoughtful. Bob and I just about live here and you are always kindly to us." The receptionist's eyes left her computer and met mine and the smile she gave me met my quest for the good stuff. Her words were grateful and from them I gathered that grateful patients are generally silent and the ungratefuls tend toward the snarky comment.

What a job, always being pleasant. Pleasant in patients' computerized appointment-making face to face or by phone and sometimes hectically, and silent-calm in the snark attacks. I was glad to have mentioned my thanks. These few words softened the day. *The First in my search*.

In a nano second I turned and found myself exiting along with the odd-noises elder in her wheelchair. But the wheelchair occupant was neither an elder nor a she. He was a young boy with arms waving wildly and a mis-formed body harnessed in for safety. Of course it was to me to hold the door for the aide and the boy.

"I will be your door person," I announced, amidst the action. To the boy I said, "It was good to see you today," this to a boy never seen before nor likely ever again, but I felt like saying it so I did. No response was discernible or expected, but the moment was quietly good.

To the beautiful aide I said, "Thank you for your help," because while I held one end of the door for her she smiled and held the other for me. Silver senior me, walking with a quirky-knee limp. It was one of those dear small exchanges. Perhaps not everything is terrible after all. Decency lives. Here was a *Second self-serving of decency* right on top of the first.

And there were more, that day and the next and the next. A days-long path of uplifts, it turned out to be.

On a different doctor-day of blinding downpour – the sort that swells mighty Midwest rivers – Bob and I left safe home in mere overcast. En route we encountered flash-flooded streets, also unprecedented for our Northeastern town, and we arrived with the torrents.

No blue-striped parking spaces meant we would drench ourselves en route to the In door, which is OK. But out of nowhere came greeters with sky-blue hoodie ponchos and matching giant blue umbrellas. *Here was Good*

Stuff Three. They were all over the place, these rescuers in blue, and whose idea it was I do not know.

What I do know is that having these good souls there with a wheelchair for Bob and an umbrella for both of us was a surprise of kindliness. Thanking them was easy and we did it over and over. There it is again, the Thank You thing. Self-serving behavior, saying thank you and meaning it and warmed by the smiles of response.

Other events: Some heavy-machinery workers ripped out a key tree root to upgrade our neighbor's driveway. Elegant Belgian block apron in the works. I could see the hefty severed eight-inch diameter root six feet long, nutritionally and structurally essential for the health of the tree, as had long been discussed over our shared privet hedge. The tree is dear to us, one of four glow-in-the-Fall maples that we planted years ago when our children went off to college. Town-owned curb trees all along, yes, yet planted by us and long loved by us.

My afternoon anger at our neighbor was soft-voiced but unsuppressed, and witnessed by the workers with shovels stilled. Workers who had been helping me back out of my driveway that morning amidst the chaos of bulldozers and loud-pounding earth-movers. Workers who had been following someone else's customary instructions all day, details all unbeknownst to us next door.

I dealt with neighbor-anger as needed for my own calming. The deed is done. Let it be. Rage cooled to zero in a few hours.

Next day I walked over to the men doing the work. Morning's wisdom to self: leave it alone. My anger was for my neighbor, I said to them, not for their own good work. One man – the one in the white tee-shirt who also spoke the best English – kept saying "I'm sorry, I'm sorry," and I said "Please, no need for you to be sorry, thank you for your help to me with my car." The smiles returned, the workers' and mine. What perceptions had each taken home last night, after the bitter words witnessed near the splendid young maple tree at their work site?

A Good Morning talk with the driveway guys – self-serving, self-calming words of thanks again. *A Fourth Good-Stuff occasion.*

That week I also elicited a smile from a harried mustachioed clerk at the DMV when I renewed my driver's license. *That's Five.* And I wrote "Margaret is terrific!" on an attentive waitress's dinner check. *Six.* And, I wished that EZ Pass had not done me out of pleasant-greeting smiles from toll collectors. Unrewarding task, theirs, with driver rudenesses punctuating every shift. A Seventh Self-Serving "friendly hello" exchange, no longer the common occasion of years ago. *I will count it Seven in recollection.*

But then I thought of Brian the mailman – he has a tiny daughter named Daphne and gladly showed me her photograph when I asked. I see him pretty much every day. ... And the little rainbow rock from my granddaughter. ...

Well, I can still be as deeply grouchy as the next. No change there. But a smile offered and answered: priceless. So easy. So healing of the thirsty spirit. ❖

Boy and Ducklings at St. John's Pond

"Oh, look!"
A little shorts-and-blazer-clad boy
stood at the pond's split rail fence,
pointing wide-eyed to ducks and ducklings
before entering the church beside the pond.
Parents and baby brother were close by.
Church before church.

Mr Forsyth's Forsythia

Once, a few pre-pandemic years ago, spring sprang right along without me. I lost five days to the flu – heir to the Spanish Influenza devil that killed forty million people in 1918, and thousands more a century later, in sudden strikes. Flu vaccine, doctors, and miracle pills saved me from all but the first dreadful day. The sixth day gave me forsythia, as if brand new.

On a first tentative venture around the block on Day Six, I came upon forsythia in full sunny morning glory on neighboring lawns. Last time I had seen, it was just suggestion. But this time it was fulsome – already showy yellow, with purple rosebud and daffodils and hyacinths its only rivals thus far. All else was merely on the verge.

How could it be, I marveled, that only then, only this first time ever, did I notice two differing forsythia yellows? One was lemony, the other gold. Small difference, quiet revelation. I am the only person in the world who never knew.

Forsythia has always charmed my heart with its boldness: *I'll be bright before anyone else. It's OK that nobody notices me anymore once the grass greens and the leaves come out. I've had my time.*

Crocuses and snowdrops have the same brief glory, earlier and tinier. And like them forsythia forgives and comes again the next year and the next no matter who noticed or did not. Beautiful, self-confident little blossoms.

So where did forsythia, so forgiving, come from with such confidence?

In England it is "for-sigh'-thia," long i sound as in high, for its naming after Scottish botanist William Forsyth, 1734-1804. (Not to be confused with William Forsythe, b 1978, who portrays handsome gangsters in the movies. An extra e in my online search sent me astray at first.) And before England, forsythia's home was the Far East – a member of the olive family Oleaceae. Exotic pedigree.

Forsythia's Forsyth was famed for his dissertations on fruit tree and forest tree illnesses, and was furthermore a Founding Member of the Royal Horticultural Society and Royal Head Gardener at the palaces of Kensington and St. James. Ladies likely found him handsome in his day – white hair curled at the sides, gentle expression, high collar and lacy cravat of the era. His forsythia reached European gardens by mid-nineteenth century and American hybrids arrived around the time of World War I. So our friendly forsythia hasn't always existed in the United States. Yet it seems native, a forever thing.

One online glimpse at forsythia's flowering confirmed the limit of my knowledge: a childhood, and ever since, loving the daring yellow first to follow the whites and purples of snowdrops and crocuses. Online I saw – and fled – Garden Shoppe videos and treatises on the infinite varieties of hybrids and styles for this or that placement. Gardening columns wax eloquent on the quirks of this plant I have loved for its plain beautiful ways.

Horticulturalists at Yale and Harvard and varied erudite sites – more staid – extolled virtues and traits: Loves full sun … carefree maintenance … branches bow down gracefully toward the ground … cut out one quarter of largest-oldest stems at ground level each year … trim branches back just after flowering, because buds begin to form then for the burgeonings of spring.

And this upbeat summation from the Arbor Day Foundation: "Fast growing hardy shrub providing a sunny sight before the rest of the landscape greens up."

But the best remark came from an impassioned man named Eric Larsen at the Marsh Botanical Garden at Yale, in a lyrical video on forsythia care. Rounded or squared forsythia shrubs, "stifling the graceful natural arches of the forsythia branch," he declared, "are gauche." And "If it ever comes to

pass that you trim your forsythia into geometric shapes," he promises,
"I'll find you, I'll come to your house late at night and hide your pruners."

So I stayed away from the plenitude of forsythias in today's splendorous garden shops – I even saw my old friend humiliated as a hedge. How awful.

And instead I discovered late in life that there are lemon and gold versions. That I'm not alone in my lifetime of love of forsythia. And that the elegant bowing-toward-the-ground arch is held sacred by others as well. ❖

My Morning Walk

My morning walk shifts with the seasons, the day, the time of day. It is a mix of sights and sounds and insights, never twice the same. Sometimes it is so bracing and beautiful I say hello to the air.

I walk in my neighborhood, same blocks, same two miles. I know it well – fifty years of noticing the progress of forsythia, the stage of magnolia blossoms, the green or brown of lawns, the coming leaves or still no leaves at all and the sharp lines of trunks and limbs reaching all the way up.

I know the houses too: a second story added, a young tree planted, a side lot sold off, a wheelchair ramp gone, no longer needed when a young boy and his family move away. And I know some of the children – balloons here for birth or birthday or graduation, hockey sticks clacking in the street, baskets swished or missed in the driveway. Neighborhood – the word speaks. Here is a life of belonging, working, sharing intimacies when we are out walking our dogs. There is no medicine like it.

Today's walk was still winter, twenty-one degrees and sunny and windy a bit. The rhododendrons have curled their leaves tight against cold. Black ice lies in wait. My defense is hat, jacket, gloves, good shoes, and a purple knitted neck warmer from my son in law: just an eight-inch-tall column of scarf that slips on before and below my hat. It keeps the wind from sneaking down my jacket collar, and I can pull it up over my face if the wind bites.

Outside, there's my street – the same next-door houses, sidewalks, gardens still crisply bordered (not my gardens!), fences mended, lawns trim under patches of snow. Down the way and around the corner there's the untended yard that has snaggly shrub roses pink all over in spring.

I remember an upstart sapling just down the street from the lilies of last year, daring a three-foot protrusion up through a Rose of Sharon bush; it stood tall and lasted long weeks till lopped into conformity. Brave sapling!

And I remember a day near there thirty years ago, in my running days. Our dog Jake ran with me – graceful beautiful black lab, joyous in his front-yard trespasses and back and forths, adding laps so as not to outrun me.

A man came out of his house: "Keep your dog off my property."

I apologized, said we'd try.

"Just keep your dog off my property," came next.

On I went with my shiny joyous Jake. A car came alongside, slowed. The property man, following me. Defending his diminutive white ranch house now downhill from us. Black car, too close to me, elbow out the window in an I-mean-business kind of way. Same demand.

"Do you truly want to keep saying this to me, when I tell you that my father died this morning?" I asked him.

"Just keep your dog off my property," he said.

My father had actually died the day before – too much truth for a car window exchange – I had held his hands and wished him well. The sweet peacefulness of his death was with me at that black car moment. It has stayed with me forever, undamaged by this man's words.

On other mornings I love seeing the eagerness of two dogs I meet on the way – Charley, black-white, furry, and later Lady, small, trim, tan – each leashed and tail wagging. A baby carriage too – there's no way I can get by without seeing the tiny face inside. After all, I'm a grandmother. Sometimes the innocence hurts my heart – the world is so troubled now and these little persons will inherit it.

But then along the way come the crocuses and snowdrops of early March –

daring little things so OK with being nipped in the bud. Their color cheers –
white, green, palest purple, tiny and grand. There is hope.

Notable on these morning walks, whatever the season, is that fresh
thoughts are free to come. It is an inward-looking time. Yes, sometimes
despair comes. Then resolution for action. And yes, a litany of missed
intentions, then grit for the elusive errand or call. I come home with energy
to knock everything off the list.

And the sounds one particular morning after black-ice days – soft-voiced
doves, a chittering crowd of starlings, no robins yet. But a woodpecker in the
same old tree. I admire the speed of his beak-peckings – how does he do that?
Why doesn't his head hurt? I'm surely not the first to muse about this.

Oh, and the winter-spring nor'easters we've had recently here in our
savored Northeast – three in two weeks and another in the offing. Earth
retaliates for our mindless climate sins. Flooding rains and thundersnow.
Branches down all around – no big ones, no power-outing ones. Just old limbs
pruned by God. Today on my walk I look up to see where the limbs came
from, the freshly naked limb remnants up above.

The evergreens lost the most greenery – needles caught the wind when
bare trees had no leaves to take? Most yards have evergreen sprigs sprinkled
across them or already gathered at the curb. Still green, the needles, all that
work year after year, gone for naught. Some budding branchlets of maple
are down too – too soon for their grand spring intentions.

In one yard I see snow plow gouges rending the tended lawn. In another
I see dormant gardens, bedded down but getting ready. Down the way I
see pale tan zoysia grass behind a tan split rail fence – the old fellow and his
small grey terrier say hi with waves and a tail. And I see old boards edging
what I know is a tiny tomato garden – green stalks will be staked and full
come summer. Each sight slips into brain-file for a later time.

Sometimes on my morning walks I'm so lost in thought I end up well along in my routine of streets. How can that happen?

Perhaps it is the same as sleep, that way of being – it knits up the ravel'd sleeve of care. That's how it feels to me. ❖

BESSIE FUCHS

Out for a Walk Today

Out for a walk today
Mid February 60° yesterday
Blustery 27 today
Confusing
Birds are back, chirps
Sticks and cones strewn on lawns,
Nature's pruning
Met a man walking his dog
The dog stopped to sniff
and listen to everything -
Every inch, every tree,
Rhododendrons unfurling
Shrub roses eager
Every living thing
Hoping for hints of spring.
It was wondrous.
Said the man
Of his dog's elation,
"It's like for us being on top
of a mountain seeing beautiful things,
feeling heady. That's how it is for a dog."
I had never thought of it that way.

Dirt Resplendent

Today after the stops
and starts and freezes
of almost spring, I passed
a lawn space now pure dirt.
Trees down and all else
bulldozed blank and bare.
However, a sprout of purple
caught my eye. A crocus!
And then another and
a whole string of them!
Not opened yet but daring
and promising in the surrounds
of dirt. "Hear ye! Tiny hiding bulbs
best the Goliath dozer!"

After a Time of Tears

I sit out with Serena Frog
After a time of tears
My wine and I sat outside together.
I noticed light spring blue sky and
White happenstance clouds.
What a marvel to see maple bracts,
Soon leaves, presenting themselves
On the tiniest branches.
What are the names of things
All around me? I tried to remember
The beautiful old-friend names . . .
Andromeda
Bridal veil
Boxwood
Rhododendron
Lavender
Shrub Rose
Dusty Miller
Hemlock
Magnolia, blossoms spare and spent
After lush early daring.

Dogwood, no flowers yet but
Pink-blossomed in my memory.
Oh I wish my sister were here –
This dogwood is for her.
Oh how I wish I could tell her
Of recent frightening planetary days.
Of hope wished for, of the
Flowering Pear across the street:
Spring's frilly white statement of gaiety?
The old bench I lean back on
Is still a deep lasting dark green,
After seasons and seasons of comfort.
Isn't life something?
Perhaps I am invisible on my porch,
Wine and solitude in springtime -
How pleasing to imagine so.
Tonight, beautiful end of day,
Gentle after a time of tears.

Goings and Comings

Yesterday I attended a memorial service for a friend. A dear white-bearded friend and shipmate and solid source of comfort in low times and a fellow celebrator in high. Words of praise and love flowed in all hearts that day – kindness, generosity of spirit, love of and by children and grand-children, friends, fellow sailors and singers. Adventurous intellectual life – bright mathematician and rich bass in our choir for twenty years. Growling loving grandfather. Of course I thought of my own life, our children and grandchildren, the rains of blessings in our own hard times, the essential ease of our own entire lives. And now I ponder yesterday today, ensconced in the local library, editing poetry for a fine client age ninety-three.

Daydreaming for a moment, I think of my lost friend and his gifts to my life. I think of the adventures and high times with so many friends, now missing also yet somehow still part of my life. How does all that work?

My parents, sister, and brother have all died. I am now older than any family member ever came to be. The other day, on a whim, I listed my losses to death – quite a list by now and starting early. And I noted who on the list I truly missed in my life today – my heart told me the ones. Time winnows things, I found. Essential connections sort themselves out with death – some stay richly full and some distill to a single precious moment.

Among my early losses are childhood and high school friends and college classmates. Later, colleagues and clients at work, church choir friends and tennis and sailing sparring partners, neighborhood friends of all our family. Each has nourished me with affection and shared understandings. Each left too soon, from teens to eighties. It seems always too soon of course – unless with illness and pain death becomes blessing . . . the comforting "peace at the last."

The ones who died (suicide, accident, illness, murder, nature's time) exist warmly. They are gone from daily thought, but certain times with each still sculpt me, still guide my sense of things.

Sometimes I count up these plentiful Goings. How do my losses match up to the Norm of Losses? Yes I do have my fair share. And then I come upon the Comings – the sustaining souls who have entered my life over time and stayed there alive and well. That list is marvelous and likely just like anyone else's.

But here is how I see mine: My garden of friends is both annual and perennial – cold (absence and silence) takes some and all the others keep their colors, ready for spring. Joy, light, dark times shared in walks, calls, letters, book recommendations and conversations, a glass of wine in sadness, gladness, serious stuff, tomfoolery. The soul-to-soul stuff of which sustenance is made. All this from the seeds planted over time, the Comings and Stayings.

Leaving church one Sunday recently, not long before yesterday's service for my white-bearded friend, I came away with a sweet sense of wellness. It was not the sermon, which was surely fine. Or the hymns, yes consoling in their messages and familiarity. It wasn't even church itself, with the people I greet and the place I always like to sit – far back on the right.

It was something else. It was the sense of interconnection of spirit that the morning itself had awakened. The Goings-Away of friends lost, refreshed by the Comings-In of friends found over time. Intangible, beautiful.

Yet there are still other friends that lend strength to well-being, I realize. Ones neither met nor lost. Friends found in books. I think of Kahlil Gibran's philosophy – of the shared intimacy of minds. His words guide me every day in saying thank you to the plumber, mailing a letter and saying hello at the local post office, finding true conversation at a cocktail party. And I think of C. S. Lewis's *Shadowlands* recognition – that we read to know we are not alone. So it is not just the friends we meet and walk with. It is also the friends whose words we can walk with at any hour of the day.

Later that Sunday of well-being, over a second cup of coffee, I glanced at my little rough-hewn wooden statue of St. Francis, bird on shoulder as is always his fashion, and noticed his hands. Hands held heavenward in prayer, of course. But I had never recognized the other message of the hands. The unspoken word from this peaceful man to me: Namaste.

Namaste: In all of life's goings and comings, I greet you. Yes. ❖

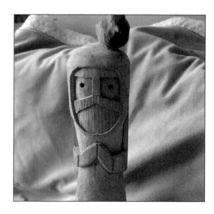

Aging in Place II

Aging in place
Forever a dream
Now a demon.

Once,
Nestlings fledged,
Chair committees
Help the world
Weep at weddings
Hold first grandchild
Welcome wisdoms
Tidy up DNRs and wills.

Then one morning,
Winter.
Death of friends
Lurk of senility
Ache of bones
Love letters for loss
Dark Day.
Whither from here?

Thus this morning,
Mourn? Or
Walk, notice snow drops
And forsythia and buds
Admire saplings and
Volunteer maples
Send love letters for thanks
Breathe, sigh, pray.

Check the Trees for Squirrel Nests!

Take a moment now while the weather
is more brisk than shocking,
to check the trees for squirrel nests.
With leaves full gone you can find them –
bunches of sticks and leaves in the crook
of a branch, near the tops of the tallest trees.
Lest these perky creatures winter over
up there, snow-covered, tossed by freezing wind,
they generally leave these summer homes by now
in favor of a hollow tree trunk. Miracle!

Stanley Smiled

One day in April I met a man named Stanley, at the local fresh food deli counter. My spirit was weary. Impatience and annoyances had colored the day dark. Likely it was raining too – sure should have been. The quiet of morning had missed its calming chance. Serotonin-upping behaviors at the Y – didn't happen. Life's daily trail of doctor appointments, age appropriate aches and pains, and searching yet again for lost belongings was winning the day. I set out for some essential errands in a grouchy grandma attitude.

Bananas, yogurt, avocadoes, tomatoes, bread, butter, eggs. I thought first of that fresh-baked sourdough loaf all rounded with ornamental pre-baking slits in the crust. That new favorite discovered at my health-conscious daughter's house – the preferred bread of our young granddaughters, who were coming to visit soon.

So to the bread and deli section I proceeded. There was nobody at the racks of freshly baked breads, so back behind the tallish counter I went to read labels and find my new favorite. There it was.

"You can't be in here," said a man's voice. Quiet, pejorative.

No "May I help you?" No "Sorry, Ma'am, but ..." Just peremptory words by a pony-tailed stranger in a crisp white apron.

"Sorry, I didn't know," said I. Truthfully. The man took the bread and bagged and tagged it. Mentioned the Board of Health regulations. Pointed to a sign I had not seen, intermixed with a full row of other things ranged eye-height along the counter top.

Then deli-rage hit me. I moved the sign to the end of the counter. "I moved the sign so people can see it," I said in snidest fashion (holding back tears; grouchiness had triumphed over composure). And headed away.

Then righteousness hit me. I turned back and leaned an elbow over the high counter and said, tears all too near: "You know, you really don't know what troubles other people may have."

Silence. Then, from Bread Man, whose name I would learn is Stanley: "Yes, you're right. I have cancer."

Stunning.

Whereupon we had a conversation, Stanley and I, about difficulties and blessings. Here was one of those gifts that comes from nowhere at the just-right moment. Kindness on a fraught day. Stanley saw my incipient tears and offered a smile. I learned of the spread of his cancer. He heard of my concerns. We philosophized. We touched each other's spirits in the small deep way that just sometimes happens.

Then he came out from behind the counter and stood there, arms at his side and the white apron now endearing, and said, "Would you like a hug?"

"Oh, yes," I said.

And we exchanged a hug, Stanley and I, that mended a day once broken and now made whole. ❖

The Dancing Leaf

This morning I woke up somewhat grouchy –
nothing was pleasing and things weren't going my way.
So I went out for a walk, and came upon a dancing leaf.
It seemed like magic – a cheery autumn-colored leaf,
all orange, picked up by the wind and dancing around.
But here's the magic part – the leaf kept on dancing,
two feet off the ground, two feet below a pear tree branch.
It was a maple leaf, caught on an invisible spider-thread,
dangling down from a branch, caught fast and still there,
dancing around, when I came back from my walk.
I told no one about it till now.

The Lightening

Go downstairs for sunrise! It is almost time. . . .
I woke up with this incentive today, this wish to begin
the day alone in quiet splendor. It was 5:55 a.m. on
Tuesday December 7th, 2021, in Cold Spring Harbor.
Morning coffee and sunrise are among treasures life
offers me every day, at grateful age eighty and some.
Later, my cellphone will shatter peace with the news of the day.

From my chair, coffee in hand, I begin to see rhododendron leaves, maple
tree branches barely stirring in lacey silhouette, and first light over the rooftop
of a neighbor's house across the street. Sunrise is at 7:05 today, and before that
the dawn begins at 6:34 – two different accountings of the start of today, of
every day. Delicious when you think of it. There will be 9 hours 20 minutes of
daylight today, a minute or so fewer than yesterday. We are nearing the dark
of the Winter Solstice.

A glance away from morning thoughts and now a soft suffusion – the sky
is light blue with swishes of peach striation sky wide. What a beginning!
I think about recent moments out and about in our neighborhood, where I will
soon be having a morning walk. I may see Copper, Cooper, Arthur, Olive, or
Opal, dog friends of mine.

I may see a baby in her cozy carriage, and mention the wonder of it to her
parents, who already know.

I will crunch through maple leaves and pear tree leaves and, finally, the last
leaves of the old recalcitrant oaks. (Acorns fell for the squirrels in September.)

I will perhaps see my neighbor Richard out raking his yard; his late wife
had a birthday the exact same day as mine. He and I are elders born in the exact
same year, 1940.

Every day in our neighborhood, every morning or afternoon walk, brings
these shining moments. Infinitely. ❖

They Taught Me How to Love

When my brother Hal died recently, a fresh question came: Am I an orphan? Our mother, father, and sister had died long before. So I looked it up: qualifications for being an orphan. * Well, I don't have those qualifications: you must be a minor to lose your family, to be the last one standing. So I am not an orphan. I am a wife-mother-grandmother just past eighty, gratefully all, but no orphan. * But wait. Yes I am contentedly settled, with husband, children, and grandchildren. But what about being not lonely but the lone tree standing in my founding family forest? * When we were very young, we were five in number. I was the completion, the last born, the first to bed, the baby, the sheltered one. We were five and today we are one. * What I do still have is a trove of family memories, and last glimpses of each of these four who preceded me in life and in death. Beautiful glimpses, actually. Dear finalities. * Life and loss are tough-love teachers, aren't they? I lost my the four of my founding family, and each one, in my myriad memories, taught me how to love.

The teaching continues. Christmas 2021 kept distance yet brought post-pandemic hope. And, presents of a non-store-bought sort. Pandemic hope. And, presents of a non-store-bought sort. Mine were delivered with this note, beginning *"To Dearest All, in reverse order by age"* - see facing page -

Gifts to faraway you of some books that I love
and of some moments that I remember way down deep –

To Brooke – The picture of tiny baby you in my care, lying on the floor
all in a pink onesie, when you and Paige and your mother and I were
looking around Bridgehampton. You laughed and laughed,
and I remember sitting on the floor talking to you and telling you
that I loved your smiles and your kicky little feet.

To Paige – My book *Misty of Chincoteague*, a gift to me from
your great grandmother Jenifer, when I so loved horses.
She arranged for us to have lunch with the author, Marguerite Henry.
Later my sister and I – your Aunt Elizabeth whom you never got to meet –
drove down the coast to Charleston and en route
we did see the shaggy ponies of Chincoteague Island!

To Jake – A photograph from the day you and I went around
your Wakeman Road circle looking for beetles and worms.
We counted them carefully on our piece of white notebook paper,
and made a report for your parents. You were skilled in looking
under rocks and finding tiny scurrying creatures
wishing we would let them be, which we did, and gently so.

To Graham – A picture of my pine cone Thanksgiving turkey
on brown pipe-cleaner legs, a fine creature made by you for school,
with my name Geema – after MomDadMatthewGraham –
on one of his five light brown paper feathers.
That turkey lives on our living room ledge
and means the world to me. I see it pretty much every day!

To Matthew – A famous book from my treasure shelf –
West With the Night by Beryl Markham. Who knows whether you will
love it as much as I did – solo flying is far from baseball and basketball
but it has everything to do with splendid writing,
and being free and strong and daring in life. Bodes well for you!

To Amy – Some draft pages of a little book I wrote years ago in the
exhilaration of becoming a grandmother, called *Letters to Matthew*.
Perhaps I will publish it someday, but for now it is about
your first-born son and my time caring for him
when you were finishing your teaching year in New York.
The preliminary cover design is how we began.

To Robert – A hefty book from a moved-away friend for you all,
about famous baseball players Daddy and I used to know.
I watched Stanley Cup hockey games with my family growing up,
but I learned about baseball from watching it
with Daddy and Jenny and you. I loved attending a Mets game
with you on Mother's Day and receiving a pink hat!
Soon . . . an amazing present TK from Daddy!

174

To Jenifer – The little red leather 1928 Prayer Book
from my mother when I was confirmed. It is crumbly-edged
not from use but from age! Rosalie Terry Slack, it says
on the cover. I think I gave you one too, marked Jenifer Slack Walton?
So now you have this one given to your mother
by your grandmother Mariamne Jenifer Houston Slack.
You two would have had a fine time discussing life!

To Tim – A book recommended by a friend – called, cryptically,
The Swerve. I am newly through it and find it provocative in the most
wonderful ways. I put little checkmarks in my margins;
perhaps we can talk about them one day.
It is about early libraries and the writings of the ancients
being forever lost to pillage and fiery volcanoes, yet found in scroll
fragments breathtakingly lucid and relevant for today.

To Bob – The draft of my Dedication to you in the incipient
Prickly Garden book, headed (in hope) for publication in the next year
or so – well past its intended completion date at age 80 for me!
My poems and vignettes reflect adventurous and challenging times
in the past two pandemic years, and the knowledge and confidence
and joy I have found in my 56 years with you.
You also, perhaps above all, have taught me how to love. ❖

Also by Terry Walton –

Cold Spring Harbor Daybook

Cold Spring Harbor – Rediscovering history in streets and shores

Hello, It's Me – A memoir of good events, and some that seemed otherwise at the time

Kindnesses – A journey through the seasons of grief in poems, prayers, and joyous observations

Harbor Voices – New York Harbor tugs, ferries, people, places, & more

Colophon – A Note on the Typeface

Palatino Linotype – odd name, and what is Linotype anyway? Linotype was the brilliant metal typeface scheme of ages ago, whereby hot lead was formed into letters and jingled down a chute to form words in a wooden type drawer (galley), first in a single line of type and onward in paragraphs and pages. Proudly I state that years ago as an editor in the 1960s I worked in Linotype. All pre-digital everything. My magazine was the first to use computer page makeup, using digitized alphabet characters. Fond memories, those. So, my affection for this beautiful typeface Palatino Linotype is history-born. ✳ Palatino typeface entered present-day omnipresence in 1948, the work of noted calligrapher Herman Zapf (1918-2015). But go back way further to namesake Giovanni Battista Palatino (1515-c1575), a contemporary of Leonardo da Vinci and a master calligrapher in Rossano, Calabria, a town in Southern Italy today known for its alabaster and marble. ✳ I have loved this graceful old-style serif typeface for years, an elegant competitor to tried-and-true Times New Roman. So, I chose Palatino for this *Prickly Garden* book – with the blessing of the book's delightful designer Eric Neuner.